Standing with the Dog

K-9 Kampus

Standing with the Dog

K9 Psychology in a Nutshell

K-9 Kampus

Mel Helmick

Standing with the Dog
By Mel Helmick

Printed in the United States of America

ISBN 978-0-9816511-5-6

Note: This publication contains the opinions and ideas of its author. It is intended to provide helpful and informative material on the subject matter.

Standing with the Dog: K9 Psychology in a Nutshell
is a publication of:

Stand a Chance Publishing
Hot Springs, Arkansas 71901

www.standingwiththedog.com
www.k-9kampus.com
https://www.facebook.com/pages/Mel-Helmick/271361106263294
https://twitter.com/#!/MelHelmick

Acknowledgments

I once read that the most important page in a book is the Acknowledgments. The reason for this is that each acknowledged individual has inspired each page of the book. With this in mind, though there are so many who deserve recognition, I will keep this as short as possible.

I would like to thank my Dad for being so supportive throughout my life's journey. Thanks for being there for me Dad. To my grandparents, you have taught me so many of the most important things I have learned in life. To my children, Jonathan, Wade and Josh; boys, thank you for your patience and understanding. Never stand down.

I would also like to thank our church, Sulphur Springs Missionary Baptist Church. God has blessed my family with each of you.

I would also like to thank the following people who, throughout my life's journey, have been blessings. You have not only provided education on various levels, but also served as a tremendous source of support, guidance and strength: Mike and Donna Hunter, The Yerger family, Matt Hammond, Jonathan and Krystle Mize, Heath Farthing, Dayton Waters, Julie Kreth , Karen Ragsdale (ARRUFF Rescue), Larry and Iva Rice, Connie Davidson, Karen Odom Burkley Kovacik, and Jim Kochenburger, I could not have done this without you.

I would like to thank Janet Bailey and Linda Lipe for introducing me to my first encounter with a bait dog, and for providing me with hands-on experience and exceptional knowledge. They have not only assisted me in my journey in the Animal Cruelty and Neglect industry, but in numerous other ways throughout my career as a whole.

I would also like to acknowledge the many dedicated and responsible dog owners, breeders and trainers who take a stand with the dog every day. A special thanks to Mike Yarnell, an outstanding breeder/trainer of German Shepherd dogs. Thank you for providing me with an awesome partner, Tisha.

I would like to acknowledge and thank the many individuals who lost sleep last night due to the cruelty and neglect cases that swarm through their every thought. To those who spend their free time trying to make the world of a dog a better place to be, I thank you for standing.

Last, but definitely not least, many thanks to each of the numerous clients and dogs I have been blessed to work with. I am thankful also for the many dogs I have encountered in my life, particularly those that serve our country. Thank you for standing and teaching us, by exhibiting leadership, guidance, grace, compassion and understanding.

There exists but one
unsurpassed dog trainer,
the dog.

Introduction

Over the last several years, many attendees who have attended various levels of training with K-9 Kampus have requested that I comprise a book or curriculum. The idea was to create a forum for sharing insights on the ideology and methodology of canine interaction I have taught in my programs over the years. On numerous occasions, it has also been suggested that if I chose to embark on such an endeavor, it could be of great benefit to direct such a book to the Shelter/Rescue/Animal Cruelty and Neglect industry. While this has been a primary focus for me as I wrote this book, I have also tried to gear the content to our society in general. My hope is that readers will gain a better understanding of the animals involved and that the community of animal specialists would be drawn closer together, working together as a team on a solid foundation.

Standing with the Dog K9 Psychology in a Nutshell, is the beginning of series of books. Others will follow that will lead, guide and direct you through many of the various training curriculums in dog world today.

By reading this book, I believe you will glean useful information that will clear up any pressing issues you have with your dog and that you will enjoy an even more fulfilling relationship.

Contents

Important

Throughout this book, when the word "handler" is used, it applies to and includes anyone who works directly with a specific dog or dogs, or who may be otherwise involved in the K9 industry. This includes, but is not limited to: those who operate within a shelter/rescue environment, caretakers, volunteers, animal cruelty investigators, management or board members of such organization, as well as breeders, trainers, veterinarians, veterinary assistants and private dog owners.

Chapter One

Prerequisites for the Handler

First and foremost, potential handlers must ask themselves why they want to own a dog, or work and volunteer in any of various fields of canine caretaking or handling. Regardless of whether this handler is the owner of the dog or working as a business owner, volunteer, or as compensated staff, consideration must be given to: the accompanying sacrifice to family; the amount of time, effort, energy, and money required for adequate shelter; proper care, training and continuing education for both dog and handler. With these considerations in mind, the answers as to why one would want a dog or enter into a specific field of canine service are as varied as the ones giving the answers.

Once the reasons behind an individual's desire to own a dog or to operate in the field of canine care or handling are established, there are three prerequisites that handler must fulfill. As these prerequisite criteria are presented, it is easy see and understand how they tie together. For the candidate handler to prove successful in the field, he or she must fulfill all of these criteria. Even lacking one will most likely lead to failure.

Desire

Desire is the extent or level of willingness the handler exerts to perform certain duties. This desire must be full, complete and honest. The handler must make the decision and accept the responsibilities of entering into the decision on his or her own. If the candidate's decision is coaxed, chosen in order to appease someone else, or made simply to obtain membership in one more civic or social organization, he or she will not put forth the 100% effort required. If the candidate is given a dog as a pet, but is not thrilled about it, most likely the dog won't be either. Such a candidate will lack the desire required to succeed as a handler.

Even

If a prospective handler has any other motivation or ulterior motive that falls short of 100% commitment and desire to succeed, then they are not exhibiting the trait of being "even."

Essentially, being "even" means the individual has "nothing to prove."

The individual exhibiting the "even" trait will not only appreciate the dog under his or her care, but also recognize the benefits they can offer the dog as well as the benefits the dog can provide them.

Dedication

The amount of time, money, and effort required to obtain prerequisite training and competency to perform the many tasks required to handle dogs successfully demands a level of dedication much higher than merely taking on a hobby. In addition, the handler must be truly dedicated to dealing with the dogs on a level the dogs can understand. The handler must also be dedicated to sharing proper education with coworkers, subordinates, clients or anyone else involved, as to the successful handling, housing, training or breeding of dogs.

In a commercial operation, handler must also exhibit a high level of dedication to the organization. They must be willing to assist in training evolutions for new employees and the volunteer staff, as needed. Truly dedicated Team members must constantly seek to improve their own facility and skill set as well as the skill sets of those with whom they work.

The handler must also show this dedication to his or her primary charge, the dog. They must first and foremost, look after the animal's safety, security and welfare on a day-to-day basis, and not just during special occasions.

Chapter Two

Prerequisites for the K9

Just as we must first qualify the handler before any actual interaction or work with the dog begins, the dog must also be qualified. By doing so, we gain a better understanding of the dog's attitude and aptitude, as well as the particular drives, traits and characteristics the animal may possess. Once gained, this understanding of a particular canine will greatly assist with the proper placement of it into an environment that will be complimentary to its disposition. This affords the dog an optimal opportunity for positive growth within the environment.

The nomenclature of these prerequisites for the dog is the same as for the handler, but applies a bit differently to the dog.

Desire

Desire refers to drives, traits, and characteristics of the dog. Desire is characterized by the dog's drive to play, learn and work. The dog that is constantly excited to play (bringing the handler toys, etc.), or immediately eager in training situations displays a high level of desire. Desire is primarily influenced by the social skills of the dog and its willingness to interact or seek attention and approval. Constantly seeking approval is a defining characteristic because such an animal will work to the handler's satisfaction and not to his own. Training and work are inherently social activities. The dog that prefers to be left alone, a "loner," is seldom suitable for work. Also, the "loner" attitude is a general indication of poor socialization in the early formative months and is typically indicative of other behavioral and adaptive issues that would disqualify the dog from professional work.

Even

Evenness is the dog's ability to react appropriately to various stimuli in different situations. This is indicative of a dog's socialization, but it also goes deeper than that. Stable or predictive temperament, patience, attentiveness without obsession, and protection without unwarranted aggression are all examples of evenness that some dogs (even entire breeds), are simply born with. Some dogs simply do not have evenness.

Essentially, by exhibiting this level of "even", the dog simply has "nothing to prove" and is confident and comfortable. This dog neither cowers nor exhibits the attitudes of a bully. If a dog displays any other motivation or ulterior motive, then it is not exhibiting the trait of being "even."

An analogy I often use to best describe the dog that is not "even" is the high school bully. This dog exhibits a high display of violence, or may be overly aggressive. Rather than an example of a balanced, confident dog, this dog is overcompensating for his inadequacies. In short; the dog is fearful, and feels he must behave in such manner simply in an attempt to protect himself by trying to scare potential challengers. It will also take advantage of weaker peers in order to promote its personal position.

Dedication

Dedication is the dog's willingness to complete the desired task under varying conditions. A dog that is gives up quickly or gets bored quickly is likely unsuitable for in-depth training and work.

The dog must also exhibit a high level of dedication. This would be characterized by a high level of certain drives, traits, and characteristics. For example, a dog may retrieve a ball in an open area, but not retrieve it if it has entered the woods. Another dog may retrieve an object a few times, and then simply be done for the day. These are simple indications that a dog may not possess the required dedication for professional work.

This also applies to the dog's dedication to the handler. If a handler turns the dog off leash and the dog decides to run off and away from the handler, refusing to come back when called, this dog is obviously not dedicated to the handler. While most of us would consider this an obvious example, there are other, more subtle indications that a particular dog is not dedicated to its handler. For example, the dog may be evasive, but just as importantly (even arguably more so), reluctant to follow direction (defiant) or ultimately quit on the handler.

Simply put, dogs with low dedication may show desire, and enjoy interaction and exaggerated levels of play with the handler, but when the time comes to follow the handler's commands and direction, they begin to shut down. They refuse to comply, may appear lethargic, bored or excessively confused, and may even become combative with the handler.

While many cases of low dedication can be overcome with training, some simply cannot. The dog simply may not have the capacity to adopt the required level of dedication to perform at a professional level. The list of instances above that indicate a fundamental lack of dedication is certainly not all-inclusive, but simple and fast ways to determine the candidate's suitability for professional work.

Chapter Three

Prerequisites for the Team

While the word "team" in this book refers to the handler and the dog, you will find that the requirements for that team mirror the basic requirements for any viable relationship in life. As such, there is little tolerance or room for deviation from these principles. Unique to the handler/dog relationship is that only one side is capable of being false, improperly motivated or deliberately cruel; the handler. The canine has no agenda other than pleasing its handler. Understanding this firmly places the responsibility for the status of the relationship where it belongs, with the handler. The handler is responsible for everything the team and the canine do or fail to do, period.

This is considerably easier to manage than other relationships in life, but application of these principles would almost certainly help in the development of any successful relationship, whether it be with one's spouse, children, employer, employees, or even in one's relationship with God.

Communication

Communication is a two-way avenue by which thoughts, ideas, and information are exchanged. Communication with the dog is most obviously consists of verbalization (speaking) our desires in order for the dog to perform certain tasks. The dog neither understands nor appreciates the actual words or phrases we verbalize. What the dog actually begins to recognize is tone, inflection, and/or behaviors. When working with or interacting with the dog in any way, it is necessary to utilize three separate and very distinct tones in our verbalization of commands and directions.

Command or Direction Tone – This is the tone used for most direction of the dog. This tone is firm, but not overly harsh, threatening or overbearing. The goal is to achieve a level of tone that is definitive, or without question.

Reward Tone – This tone should be used only when rewarding or motivating the dog. This tone is of a much higher pitch, is very motivational, and should be easily recognizable by the dog as a positive interaction.

Corrective Tone – The corrective tone should be just that—very corrective in nature. This tone should be much more gruff than the other two, leaving no possibility of confusion with either. This tone is not meant to be demeaning or belittling to the dog. Though it should be appropriate for the offense, there should be no misunderstanding by the dog that the handler does not approve of whatever actions brought about this correction.

This is, however, merely the tip of the proverbial iceberg. Our communication with the dog also relies upon our posture, body language, voice inflection, sincerity and even our mood.

As a pack animal, the dog is dependent upon the leader of the pack, the Alpha / Beta, to establish not only the necessary parameters of acceptable and unacceptable behavior, but to also provide interaction, direction, food, and shelter. If a dog within the pack setting exhibits undesirable behavior, it is corrected by being dealt with both swiftly and justly. This correction may come directly from the Alpha or Beta, or from others within the pack that rank higher than this dog on the hierarchy scale. Once this correction has passed, the pack will resume their normal activities. There are no grudges held, and animosity is virtually non-existent.

The pack not only lives as a whole, but learns as a whole, resulting in pack growth as a whole. You will witness far fewer corrections being given in a typical pack setting of undomesticated animals that are dependent upon each other for food, safety, and the pack's promulgation, than at various training classes. The reason is simple: poor communication.

We must learn to communicate with the dog on the primal level he truly understands. Once we learn this, and then strive to maintain the understanding that every choice a dog makes is based upon previous experience, we can then begin to communicate not only clearly, but also effectively with the dog.

The dog's communication with the handler is much more than a bark or the actual performance of a desired behavior. As with the handler, the dog will exhibit the large majority of its communication through actions or reactions the novice may overlook as mere subtleties. The dog will convey its mood, confidence, desire, or fear through the use of most of its body. Most important are the dog's eyes.

The eyes present an accurate picture of the dog's clarity and focus in the requested tasking, his desire to perform it, and his reaction to a given environment. We want to see a dog that is clear in the eyes, not only from afflictions, such as conjunctivitis, but clear internally. The eyes are a window into a dog's mind and thought processes. They should convey that the dog is focused, happy, or eager to perform their work and not fearful, uncertain, or overly stressed.

In addition, the dog may also exhibit communication through a change in the setting of his ears, the bristling of his hair, the position of his head, an open or closed mouth and the positioning of his tail. It is important to recognize a combination of two or more of these changes in the dog's posture in response to a single event, environment, or stimulus. Each of these will differ to some extent from one dog to another, and must be compared against the mannerisms and body language exhibited by the dog when it is a comfortable, stress-free environment. By providing this comparison, we develop a better baseline reading of a particular dog's character, confidence, drives, stresses, fears, etc. We can then better judge his reaction(s) to the newly introduced tasks, environment or stimulus.

Trust

Trust, just as we have discussed in regard to communication, must also be a two-way avenue. It is only obtained through and a direct by-product of clear, honest communication.

The hander must exhibit trust to the dog in many ways. One fundamental example is the exhibition of trust by the handler that the dog will perform simple obedience while off leash.

The handler also trusts the dog will function within the bounds of the handler/dog relationship in such manner that the handler does not become fearful of the dog and that the dog is not defiant, evasive or overly challenging for societal position. The handler trusts the dog to prove to be a dependable protector, confidant, companion and friend—a loyal partner.

Through this process, the dog has also learned to trust the handler such that, upon exhibition of any of these particular tasks, he will be promptly rewarded accordingly, allowing the positive reinforcement of desired behaviors to continue.

For the dog, trust is also much deeper than following the given directions and commands of the handler. For the dog, trust is also comprised of the beliefs that he will receive the type of interaction normally received within a typical pack setting, and that he will not be purposefully harmed, abused, or mistreated. Trust is also comprised in the beliefs that he will be provided for by being well-fed, provided adequate shelter, and most importantly of all, treated with respect.

As this cycle grows, one can easily understand now how trust is dependent upon both the handler and the dog, each developing a trusting relationship with the other as a result of clear, concise communication between the two.

Cohesiveness

If a particular dog and handler team has established a level of clear communication, subsequently developing a mutual trusting relationship, this team begins to become cohesive, the desired ultimate level of the relationship. To begin to understand this level of "cohesiveness," we must first recognize the related term, "adhesiveness." Adhesive, simply stated, basically means one part attached to the other by means of a third component—and not typically durable. Cohesion indicates a mutual agreement and desire to perform as a unit, with shared interest in success.

Many dogs end up in shelter or rescue environments due to the fact that the vast majority of people are not properly educated to deal with their dog on a level the dog can understand. The communication is not clear, concise, or forthright. Many working K9 teams exhibit a level of adhesiveness, that is, they are stuck together by "luck of the draw" but are not solidly bonded to each other through dedication and shared sacrifice. Therefore, when uncertainties, stress or fear arise, or new working conditions or environments are introduced, the team begins to degenerate rapidly and ultimately, come apart.

The Relationship Triangle

Having covered the primary criteria for establishing a successful relationship between the dog and handler, through use of the Triangle, we can now explore these areas and how each one is dependent upon the others. (See the illustration below.)

As the illustration shows, the handler must begin with clear, honest communication. Again, the communication must be on a level the dog can digest and comprehend. It must also be conducted openly between the dog and handler.

If solid, clear communication has been utilized, one will achieve an established level of mutual trust. Once achieved, the dramatic turn towards cohesiveness in the relationship will be easily seen.

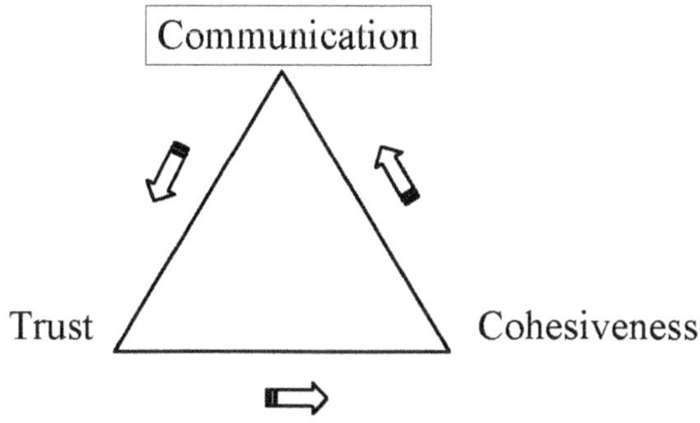

It is of paramount importance to note that this cycle should never stop. This is a continually revolving process. If continued as begun, the relationship between the dog and handler will deepen and strengthen. The level of communication, trust, and cohesiveness exhibited within their relationship will be evident, regardless of the working environment.

One can only begin the relationship development process through communication. A handler may not begin at any other point on the triangle, for without the establishment of communication, it will be impossible to develop the other two areas.

The handler should also note that if the conditioning process is begun with false, unclear, or poorly attempted communication, the cycle will not be completed. Because of the resulting conflict stemming from poor communication (or lack of proper communication), the necessary level of trust is never achieved. Failing to achieve this trust will prevent the dramatic turn towards cohesiveness.

If one were to draw this example on the previous illustration, the line leading from communication towards trust would exist, but not in context. Continued poor communication and failure to achieve the trust essential to achieving cohesiveness will continually interject conflict into the relationship. This will continue in the same direction to infinity. The triangle helps us to easy visualize how failure to establish the essential open and clear lines of communication will always result in driving the Team's relationship further and further from ever achieving the level of cohesiveness necessary to be successful.

Chapter Four

Three Ways We Deal with the K9

If we ever hope to achieve a level of success as handlers, we must understand and master the three key ways to deal effectively with the dog. The handler is the leader of the team. Leaders provide (minimally) task, direction and motivation. Obviously, the task is the action you want the team to perform. Direction sets the conditions for success, the parameters within which the team must work and the timing of the application of certain skills possessed by the team. Motivation, in terms of the K9 team, is the use of praise, reward and correction to insure certain behaviors and practices are either reinforced or discontinued. The methods by which this leadership is implemented from handler to canine are described below.

Firm

Contrary to popular belief, firm does not mean yelling at the dog, nor does it imply overly stern body language, mannerisms, or commands. Firm simply means: "Decisive or without question." By being firm, we are merely telling the dog what we expect, and that we are sure of what we want. For example, if we exhibit a questioning or begging tone when giving the dog the "Sit" command, then the dog perceives we are not exactly sure which behavior we want him to perform. Because he is not sure what we want him to perform, he will either not perform any task at all (remain standing), or out of his desire to please us, perform an alternate task (for example, to down), searching for what we may actually mean.

Compare this to someone asking you, "What color is your car?" You answer "blue," without hesitation, question, or harsh tone. The firmness with which you answered should be the level of firmness or assuredness you use when speaking to the dog. Once we achieve the mindset of giving direction clearly, in a stable, low voice appropriate for the environment, this will clear a great deal of confusion a lack of firm interjects into most training evolutions.

Fair

Fair has multiple implications throughout the conditioning process, and each will heavily influence and find reflection in the resulting outcome of the dog's training and performance of the team's mission.

Most handlers are readily prepared to deal out punishment when they believe it to be necessary. If punishment is necessary (negative reinforcement), then it should be dealt swiftly, but justly, not extending the episode unduly. Nor should the handler begin correcting with an inappropriate harshness or in a manner the dog cannot understand. More importantly, fair means that we should be even more prepared to reward appropriate or desired behavior quickly and appropriately. If this fairness is embedded in the conditioning process, not only will we have created a clearer picture for the dog of the task he is expected to perform for us, but we will also encounter fewer corrective situations. As a result, the dog will have learned what is required to please us, and in return, receives interaction, praise, and reward. This creates a more attractive and stimulating work environment for the dog and handler together, resulting in progressively fewer corrections overall

Fair also means the handler cannot constantly "change the game plan," as this will only cause confusion. If the dog is being conditioned in English, and on one day, the command to lie down is "down" and the command to sit is "sit," then on the next day, telling the dog to "sit down" is simply unfair because the command is not clear to the dog. For whether the dog sits or downs, he cannot be correct. We have clouded the picture for the dog on what we expect from him. We have also introduced confusion into the conditioning process. This leads directly into the third requirement.

Consistent

Consistency is simply a matter of wrapping the first two (Firm and Fair) together. The command for an action, task, or behavior must always be the same.

We must also be careful of the behaviors we allow. For example, if your dog is allowed to lie on the sofa when no one is there but the two of you, you have told him either directly or indirectly that this is approved, acceptable behavior. When friends or family visit, the dog will want to not only participate in the interaction, but also claim the place (the sofa) which he believes is his because he has been conditioned to get on the sofa. When you tell him "no," or that he is a bad dog for now getting on the sofa, you are definitely not being fair to him. You are being inconsistent in the behavior you allow. In the dog's eyes, you have, in fact, just moved him to a lower position within the pack and he can only associate that demotion with behavior that has been previously prescribed. By contradicting your own standards, you have laid the groundwork for violating trust, weakening an entire leg of the triangle

Chapter Five

Domestication of the K9

Opinions and theories about the timeline of canine domestication vary widely within the scientific community. That being said, no one disputes that domestication occurred thousands of years ago.

The domestication process most likely began after close examination of the traits, drives and characteristics of wolves and early man's recognition of the potential benefits of having *canis lupus* for a "best friend." These attributes, the very aspects of the animal which made them elusive quarry and even formidable adversaries, were the hallmarks of what would lend the animal to becoming the most trusted, respected, and arguably, the most cherished animals in history.

No doubt, early man saw the effectiveness of hunting in packs, working in unity for the protection and promulgation of the pack, and the need for structure in everyday life. One can wonder if the mere survival of early man was not directly related to his observation of the wolf. Although that's a neat thought, we can certainly see why he would want a best friend who came equipped with all the qualities and skills necessary for survival.

Early man readily recognized prized attributes within this animal, specifically their ability to operate as masterful hunters, their natural loyalty and the protective nature they exhibited towards those with whom they had an allegiance. Early man likely believed it to be an easy process to transform these wild animals into workers. They began removing young wolf pups from the litter at a very early age (or taking in abandoned pups), thus insuring significant human influence during the most impressionable time of their lives.

It would take more than that. What ensued was a long process of integrating this animal into the lives and homes of many generations; selective breeding and conditioning this new breed as members of the human pack. Over time, they began to serve within this new pack, just as they would within their own.

Enter, *canis lupus familiaris.*

Most likely, once the dog began to exhibit much less desire to range far from the home-site, first tasking for the dog began to be established, and their abilities were used to locate and hunt game. They assisted not only in tracking and locating the quarry, but also utilized their natural abilities to capture and kill the quarry. This was not a task taken lightly by early man, as their very existence was dependent upon the use of this quarry as food.

Introducing the dog to this event required tremendous amounts of trust between dog and man. For example, man had to trust the dog would not run off with the catch, nor challenge him over it. At this point, dog and man began to formulate their relationship as partners, mutually dependent, each learning to trust the other.

The next level of this partnership would most likely have been established by taking the dog into the workplace. For early man, this meant taking the dog along to watch over, guide, direct and protect his livestock. Livestock was extremely important, not only to provide food for the man and his family, but also to sell and trade for various wares and supplies the family also depended upon for day-to-day life. This meant that the dog not only accompanied the man in the field, but also began to follow his directions, many of these from some distance away.

Man's implementation of the dog into his daily working environment required a tremendous elevation of trust in the animal. This was trust the animal ultimately came to deserve and definitely proved worthy of.

After the dog had proved himself worthy of both the trust and responsibilities that had been laid upon him, he was introduced to living with the family. This new lifestyle entailed much more than simply living indoors. Under this new arrangement, the dog was considered an integral part of the family. Over time, the dog began to view its human family as the pack it was supposed to serve, respect and protect.

The service of the dog only increased in the working environment from there. When dogs began to be considered integral members of the family, the working relationship between the dog and handler was greatly strengthened. This relationship increased the dog and handler's ability to communicate and the level of trust placed in the dog. Increasing these attributes through a natural pack association meant not only were dog and man working together more effectively, but also more efficiently.

The increase in respect meant the dog began to not only recognize each member of the family as peers, but to also respect each one within the adjusted pack setting. This respect of each member increased as the dog's ability to understand and recognize the value of each one, and their specific designation within the pack hierarchy.

In a culmination of attributes, and as an exhibition of the dog taking its place within the family, the protective qualities of the dog may well be the most valuable trait it has brought to man. Although the guarding of livestock would be considered by many to be paramount in the dog's duties, the protection and preservation of the family rapidly became the responsibility most highly regarded. Knowing this animal had proven itself trustworthy with hunting game, guarding livestock, and living with the family, the additional level of security it provided was the very catalyst to solidify the dog's position in man's life.

It is crucial to understand that during this domestication period, devices such as choke chains, pinch-collars, and electric collars did not exist. For early man to be successful with this animal, he had to first study it before any capture and attempt at domestication. Such study brought man to an understanding of the animal's distinctive actions, body language, posturing, social interaction skills, and mannerisms it displayed within its natural environment and among its natural peers.

They learned how each wolf operated within the pack, that each had responsibilities and duties to perform that were necessary for the success of the pack as a whole. Man began to recognize specific behaviors and body language exhibited by the members of this pack.

It is most likely that man chiefly recognized the strict hierarchal structure within the pack, that each member of the pack had a clearly defined position within this structure. They also recognized the manner in which praise, acceptance and correction were dealt to subordinates within the pack, as well as the types of behavior exhibited by dogs seeking acceptance and praise from their superiors.

While the animals surely exhibited a certain level of problem solving skills, their reasoning ability was limited to short lines. More complex problems would be addressed by the dog, but only after it learned to first address the more elementary aspects of the problem. The dog then advances what it knows of the elementary aspects to work out the more intricate issues. It does so by addressing the balance of the problem in segments. So the dog engages a complex problem by solving individual segments, or smaller problems, rather than by utilizing an overall view of the problem, creating one single solution. Essentially, the dog attempts to work out a problem on its own, within its scope of reasoning. For more complex issues beyond its scope of reasoning, the dog applies patterned behavior, thus solving these larger problems incrementally.

By carefully implementing these findings into the day-to-day dealings with the dog, many became successful with the domestication process. It was most likely very evident to man that if a particular behavior or level of communication did not exist in the natural pack setting, the dog simply could not understand it. These implementations not only made life much easier for both man and dog, but were the very foundation upon which their relationship was formed.

This foundation, stemming from a true understanding of the dog, is what allowed the communication between the two to flow clearly. As this clarity increased for both man and dog, each began to fully understand his relative position within the hierarchal structure and each began to more fully understand and appreciate his required duties and responsibilities as members of this modified pack structure.

This process of domestication took place over many generations as man continued to learn more of the dog, and the dog more of the man. The working relationship between the two strengthened as a direct result of the necessity to increase the levels of communication required to live and work alongside one another.

Through the domestication process, the dog has given up his position within his normal pack in order to serve within ours. This animal has hunted, guarded, and protected for us. It has lived within the bounds of our homes as members of our families and has served us in many different venues as a service animal in specialized work disciplines.

Over thousands of years of integration and domestication, this animal has devoted his very existence to us. For this devotion, as well as to fulfill the inherent needs of the dog, we have inadvertently accepted the responsibility of initiating a certain level of interaction and respect, while creating an opportunity for the dog to achieve. The direct by-product of this devotion is that the dog has become dependent upon us.

This chapter would not be complete without addressing how we have dealt with this dependence, as well as how we have repaid the dog for his devotion.

Sadly, over the last century, the dog has become more ornamental than functional. This change of designation is simply due to our loss of respect for the dog. We have lost respect for the animal as God created it, and we have lost respect and appreciation for the service the animal has provided to us for thousands of years.

This lack of respect for the dog is exemplified in the backyards of our neighborhoods, and the filled to capacity animal shelter facilities all over the globe. Too many dogs are purchased simply because "it will occupy the kids," or to be able to say, "Hey, look what I have!" Too often, purchasers do no research into the attributes a certain breed may have to offer, nor of the special care it may require. When the decision is made to buy a dog, it more closely resembles buying a plant for the yard than taking on a living, breathing, thinking animal.

There is little to no proper education available to potential dog owners, as most people seem to fashion themselves canine experts, thinking, "everyone knows how to raise a puppy." No they do not—not by a long shot.

Puppies are typically purchased from a pet store (which may well have purchased animals in bulk from puppy mills), from a breeder advertising in the local newspaper, or adopted from a local shelter. Once purchased, the puppy is taken home by an unknowing and unsuspecting new owner who typically has no clue of the requirements and responsibilities for rearing a puppy—nor the stresses that accompany the process. The puppy is introduced to a foreign environment, and of course, is expected to have a full grasp of the English language, and to automatically understand that he should only relieve himself outside.

The new owner has no conception that the period between six and fourteen weeks of age is the absolute most important imprinting time for the puppy, during which certain stimuli and exposure must be presented to the dog, while others must not. It is not prudent to believe that just because the seller is offering these puppies at the age of seven or eight weeks of age means they are ready to face the world on their own. The breeder or seller most likely has no clue as to the benefits of allowing the puppy to remain in the litter setting until at least twelve weeks, preferably until fourteen weeks. Nor do most breeders or sellers have a clue as to the additional stimulation and imprinting the young dog should be exposed to during this window of time.

It is only a matter of time (usually a very short amount of time), before the animal is considered an inconvenience, put out in the backyard, and left to its own devices for interaction, socialization, stimulation and in establishing operational parameters. The skill set developed by this dog will have only one benefit, and it will be for the dog's best interest. At best, this dog will be left out in a fenced yard. At worst, the dog will be left to roam free, or will live its existence tied to a tree.

As this dog matures, owners will definitely encounter conflicts, as no skill sets have been developed correctly in the dog. The negative behavior the owner witnesses is that which the dog has understood to be beneficial to this point. Such dogs act out because they crave interaction.

What happens next? The dog gets a trip directly to the veterinarian's office for sterilization because if the widely held belief that surgical removal of the dog's reproductive organs will somehow magically correct any abnormalities in the dog's behavior, thus correcting the wrongs committed early in the dog's life by the owner.

Once back home, as the dog recovers from the anesthesia and the stress on his body from surgery, hopefully there is some care given to the animal. Often, this care reflects the interaction needed by the dog, and may possibly result in a more positive relationship between the dog and owner. The surgical procedure did not change the dog's outlook'—the interaction did.

After two or three days of care and quality interaction, if the dog is again returned to roam the backyard on its own or tied again to the tree, he becomes an inconvenient nuisance once again, though he is truly seeking is to repair the relationship he feels he has damaged.

Many of these issues have been, or will be discussed elsewhere in this book; however, we must acknowledge our failure as a society in how we treat these animals and the level of mistreatment we accept towards them. We breed them without conscience. We surgically alter them in an attempt to modify their behavior and mannerisms. It has even become acceptable not only to hit dogs, but to utilize choke chains, pinch collars, and electric collars to attain the ever-elusive element of control. (All day long, pet stores sell prong collars for Chihuahuas. Seriously, if you need a prong collar to walk a Chihuahua, you do not need a dog!)

At this point of man's journey with the dog, we have reached a plateau. We have caused more damage and given less respect to this species in the past one hundred years than in all of the previous thirteen thousand plus years combined. We are supposed to be more civilized people, yet we have come to tolerate nothing more than uncivilized behavior towards the dog. The results are overwhelming and painfully obvious.

As with any plateau, there are two routes we can take from here. The first is to begin to retreat, to slowly return to where the journey began. The second requires the most effort. It entails examining our journey with the dog until we pinpoint where we took the wrong turn...ad correct it. This is definitely the most positive and productive route to choose. In this second option, we can consciously work to correct what we have done wrong, while correcting the flaws in our relationship with this animal. The dog has given so much for us—we must begin to stand with the dog.

Hopefully, this chapter has provided some insight into the flawed path we have taken with the dog up to this point. By beginning to understand this, ultimately we can again earn the respect of the animal we have so disrespected. Therein, we can again become partners.

Chapter Six

Drives of the K9

"Drives," as the common characteristics and traits of dogs are often referred to, are an exemplification of those characteristics and abilities derived from thousands of years of development within the pack structure. Most true drives are primal in nature, genetically derived. The dog carries the genetic tendency to exhibit them. These characteristics may originally have been necessary to defend the pack or its individual members, to catch and provide food, or as an exemplification of social interaction.

Many of today's breeds may not exhibit a high level of certain drives, while exhibiting a heightened level of other drives. Disproportional drive levels in today's dog can be attributed to many things. Such influences may be the result of poor breeding, intentional selective breeding, or most importantly, the poor influences the dog is exposed to during the juvenile period of his life. This period is crucial in the dog's development of drives, traits, and key characteristics. In a pack setting, this would be when the dog learns how to play, hunt, and interact socially. Each resulting characteristic will be utilized throughout his life in order to eat, defend himself (and his pack), and to interact with others within the pack. The dog obtains an appreciation of approval, as well as how to exhibit such approval to others within the pack that reside lower in the social hierarchy of the pack.

A balanced exhibition of each drive, as each applies to individual dogs (and in relation to breed and age), will often serve as a window to view the dog's suitability in regard to stability, confidence, mental capacity, and the desire to serve the master, as well as the dog's understanding of approval or praise.

Prey

The "prey drive" rive is one of the most primary and often the most easily observed drive, based upon the desire to chase or catch quarry. Since the domesticated dog no longer has to hunt for his food, this drive is exhibited by the chasing of the ball, toy, etc. and will be exhibited more strongly in some breeds than others (as well as by specific specimens of a particular breed). Young dogs will most often exhibit a fair level of prey drive, though this is often diminished or even destroyed by an unknowing owner. In fact, many of today's dogs have a dramatically diminished prey drive. In large part this can be attributed to the purposeful toning down of this drive to aid the dog's suitability for the show ring, or to make the dog a more passive house pet. The exhibition of a high level of prey drive may be attributed to a dog's proper, selective breeding, as well as (and often most importantly), to the effort and care taken to develop this drive during the juvenile stages of the dog's life.

Hunt

"Hunt Drive" is an extension of prey drive. The dog exhibits hunt drive through the desire and determination to continue the chase after the prey is out of sight, or the desire to locate the prey, by either sight or smell, in order to initiate the chase and ultimately capture the quarry.

Play

"Play Drive" is based upon the societal structure of the pack. It is an exhibition of the dog's ability to interact with others within the pack and the comfort level it displays towards other dogs within the pack. It can serve as an example of their position within the social hierarchy. An alpha will express the desire to play briefly with others within the pack to show or express approval. Those lower on the societal ladder will ask the alpha to play, to both attempt to gain the favor of the alpha, and gain a higher societal ranking within the pack.

Retrieve

Though not necessarily a primary drive, "Retrieve Drive" is a secondary extension of the prey and play drives. The roots of retrieving lie in the dog's hunting for food and returning the take to the pack for consumption. By this, the dog receives approval, especially from the alpha. Short games of tug can be seen in the pack setting after the meal has been completed. The dog retrieving the toy, returning it to the owner for a brief game, then retrieving the thrown toy once again, exhibits this.

Defense

"Defense Drive" is derived, as the name implies, out of defense for one's self, pack or den against threats, either real or perceived. Each member of the pack has differing levels of responsibility in pack defense. Each member also has a certain value placed upon him by the pack, and an extent to which he will be defended. The alpha will always possess the highest protection value. The alpha will also assign a heightened protection value to a certain bitch within the pack with whom he has bred, as well as the resulting pups. He does this in order to ensure the promulgation of the pack.

Fight

"Fight Drive" is the extent, to which a given dog will engage a threat and continue the engagement until the threat has diminished. Upon catching quarry, the dog will fight it until exhaustion or until the quarry is taken.

Food

The dog becomes conditioned to perform certain tasks in order to receive food. Since all dogs like to eat, all will exhibit this to some extent, though some more than others.

Societal Drive

"Societal Drive" is the dog's exhibition of a desire to operate within a given pack structure. Within the structure, the dog understands certain responsibilities and seeks to interact with the other members of the pack. A dog with decent social drive will also exhibit a bit of competitiveness towards others within the pack—wanting to be included, to receive praise, etc.

Chapter Seven

Pack Structure

Animals live and operate in societal structures. These scales of hierarchies are just as varied as the animals they represent. There are many different societal structures, such as herds, prides, and packs, and each is very different.

Our concentration is on the dog and how its social scale is structured. Since the dog is domesticated from the wolf, we must understand the social hierarchy of this heritage.

Alpha

Probably the most often referred to and widely acknowledged position within the canine pack is Alpha (though the term "Alpha" is often misused and misunderstood). More often than not, this is applied to dogs simply because of the aggressive or dominant tendencies they exhibit.

To understand the meaning of Alpha, we must first understand the five (5) responsibilities of the alpha.

Leadership: In order for the pack to function successfully, it is essential that it have a figurehead that operates as an example and supplies pack direction and discipline. The Alpha carries these responsibilities. Not only does the Alpha lead by example, but dictates what, where, and when the pack will eat, but also determines the discipline for the pack. Even if a pack member other than the Alpha disciplines a subordinate pack member, this discipline must fall in line with the Alpha's accord on discipline.

Guidance: Guidance is just as important as leadership and must be present. Leadership outlines which actions or activities are wrong. Guidance defines not only why they are wrong, but provides direction for how best to avoid them in the future. Just as it is with leadership, guidance is best given by example.

Grace: Undeserved forgiveness. Two words, plain and simple.

Compassion: Compassion is exhibited by any long-serving Alpha. He will openly exhibit care and concern for each member of his pack, in regard to their physical well-being, their placement within the hierarchy and the individual growth and maturation of each younger member of the pack.

Understanding: Understanding is the basis for both grace and compassion, and must be present for either to exist. The level of understanding required to perform competently as Alpha is acquired through the accumulation of life experiences gained as he matures and works his way up the hierarchy ladder.

It should be easy to see that of these five attributes, only two could be the reason for the mistaken notion that antisocial behavior or violence identify Alpha. Yes, for the canine to achieve the position of Alpha, he must be both physically and mentally strong, be a strong successful hunter, and must exhibit a strong social attitude. These traits alone will be found within the balance of the pack, especially those in the higher rankings of the pack order. These five specific traits are the hallmark of Alpha.

One final note: contrary to many popular opinions, Alpha will be male. Though it is not uncommon to overhear people refer to their female as an "Alpha bitch," this is wrong. They may very well have a very strong-willed and even-tempered female, but the female cannot and will not be Alpha in the natural pack setting.

Beta

This is the canine that is second in line in the pack, and is always female. Alpha has chosen this female as his mate, but she has also chosen Alpha as hers. Beta plays just as much a part in creating this union as does the Alpha. Beta will also exhibit many of the same traits as Alpha, and will have a great deal of influence over the inner workings of the pack.

This would be the female that those using the incorrect nomenclature "Alpha bitch" would be referring to. Their dog, if actually possessing and exhibiting the necessary traits and characteristics, would be Beta.

Scout

Scout is actually a job description, not a hierarchal position. The scout is responsible for ranging ahead of the pack in search of both food and any threats that may be in the path of the pack. These scouts may range for a mile or more ahead of the pack for a couple of days at a time. Once either food or threat is discovered, they will vocally communicate this back to the pack while keeping watch over the prey or threat until the reinforcements arrive.

Sentry

Just as with the scout, this is a description of a job or tasking, not of a social position. The sentry remains close to the pack and serves as the front line of security. There may be many of these operating at one time, or just one, depending upon the size of the pack. At all times, at least one sentry is posted listening and watching for threats that may encroach on the bounds of the pack's territory.

The duties of scout and sentry are performed by each member of the pack. Since these duty assignments are not related to social ranking, members that serve as sentry one day will be given the duties of scout on the next. As scouts return from the field, their duties are taken over by a pack member that had been performing sentry duties. The returning member will then take on the responsibilities of sentry. This cycle of exchanging job tasking continues as long as the pack is in existence.

Omega

Omega is the pack member at the bottom of the social scale. This may simply be the youngest dog in the pack, the one with the least amount of life experiences to offer the pack, and/or this dog may be sick, weak, or even elderly.

This particular member of the pack may, however, be placed in this position because of antisocial behavior, or a blatant refusal to operate within the established societal bounds and guidelines of the pack. It is essential to remember that the pack depends upon the contribution of each and every member for its very existence.

If this pack member has been placed in the Omega position because of behavioral issues and the pack member continues exhibiting such behaviors, the pack will begin to shun him, which may result in being approached by the elders of the pack, led by Alpha. This confrontation will present the Omega with an ultimatum; leave the pack, or be killed.

While this may seem rash to us, the antisocial behavior exhibited by a member who does not contribute to the overall success of the pack creates a huge liability for the pack as a whole. The very existence of the pack may be placed under threat as a direct result of this behavior. Therefore, multiple opportunities are extended to the Omega to correct his activity or behavior. Once these are disobeyed or disregarded, banishment of the offending member is the only option left that would allow all involved the opportunity to continue to live.

Once banished, the pack will sever all ties with the now former member. It will not tolerate any attempts by the former member to regain interaction with the remaining members of the pack. If the Omega refuses to leave the pack, or leaves briefly and continues to return to the pack, the pack will kill him in the interest of their comminuted existence.

Lone Wolf

Though not actually a member of the pack, the Lone Wolf has become the title within the scope of the wolf that is possibly second only to Alpha in use and promotion. It would be short-sighted not to present this particular canine. This has likely been the most highly promoted and sensationalized position to attain because this one is capable of existing alone, never needing assistance or support, and self-sufficiency—he can take care of himself.

Nothing could be further from the truth. The canine is a pack animal, and as we have previously defined, this pack is dependent upon each and every member for the success of the pack. A wolf living alone cannot be successful, if not merely because of the lack of promulgation, then because of its inability to perform by itself each of the activities necessary for the pack to function.

In actuality, this lone Lone Wolf has previously been the Omega. He is now a social outcast and has been exiled to live a life as a reclusive pariah. Having disregarded multiple opportunities to correct his behavior or activities that were not conducive to successful pack operation, he was given the ultimatum to leave or die. This former Omega obviously chose to leave.

The Lone Wolf cannot exist alone and without the support of a pack. He will shadow the pack he was previously a member of, or locate and choose a different pack to follow. He may even be accepted into another pack, or possibly find a mate. One way or another he will choose another pack because it essential for his continued existence.

By following a pack, he benefits from their in-place security network. After all, he cannot be awake constantly, nor competently watch his entire environment for potential threats while awake. The scouts and sentries of the pack he has chosen to follow will sound the alarm at any perceived threat in the area. Thus the Lone Wolf benefits from their early warning system, and takes necessary precautions to protect himself.

The Lone Wolf also benefits from the pack he is following by means of location of food. As the scouts locate potential prey, he recognizes the calls given back to the pack. He also understands the hunting process for catching and taking the quarry. He will continue to shadow the pack, but he does not dare participate in either the hunt or the kill. In fact, he will keep ample distance from the pack as they eat. The Lone Wolf just hopes there will be enough left over for him to have a meal.

It should also be noted that many wolves that have been observed and labeled "Lone Wolf" were actually scouts ranging out away from the pack in the conduction of their duties. Just because a wolf may seem alone, does not make it a Lone Wolf.

From this chapter, we can clearly see there are many misconceptions in regard to the pack, pack structure, as well as to the individuals who comprise the pack. Alpha is not a ruthless dictator, nor can Alpha be a female. Beta is the top female of the pack, and is Alpha's chosen mate. Job titles are not indicative of social position, and the Lone Wolf is definitely not a lofty title to attain.

Chapter Eight

A Practical Understanding of Pavlovian Theory

Ivan Petrovich Pavlov was a Russian scientist whose outstanding accomplishments are of enormous significance to the working industry throughout the world. In 1904, he was awarded a Nobel Prize in Physiology for studies pertaining to how the digestive tract functions in humans and animals.

Pavlov developed a new way to monitor the digestive tract through the use of surgically implanted fistulas in animals' stomachs. This enabled him to study the organs and take samples of body fluids while the animal was able to function normally.

Pavlov invested countless hours of research to show that animals and humans can be conditioned to respond to a specific stimulus in a certain way. Perhaps his most widely known experiment involved his own personal dogs and a bell. Ivan found that consistently ringing the bell before feeding the dogs created a stimulus his dogs were soon conditioned to associate with feeding. As a result, every time the dogs heard the bell ring, they began to salivate; an unconscious reflex in anticipation of being fed their meal.

The theory most often cited in various facets of the dog training industry is "Pavlovian Theory." Sadly, this is also the most misunderstood and misapplied theory cited in the dog training industry. In a nutshell, "Pavlovian Theory" is simply, "the exhibition of a conditioned response to a given or know stimulus." Those involved with the training, conditioning, and handling of the dog should be familiar with Ivan Pavlov, and should understand how this conditioning process is to be applied throughout the experience of dealing with the dog.

There are three principles of Pavlovian Theory that we must establish before beginning the conditioning process with the dog.

1) What is the desired task we wish the dog to perform? (Conditioned Response)
2) How do we perceive initiating the dog's performance of this task? (Stimulus)
3) How can we achieve reproducible results? (Positive/ Negative Motivation)

In addressing these individually, as well as employing them together, one will discover how beautifully simplistic the canine's perception of the world around him actually is. To exemplify this theory, we will work through a simple conditioning scenario, first establishing the conditioning criteria.

1) Our desired task will be for the dog to sit (Conditioned Response)
2) We will use the command "Sit" for initiation of this activity (Stimulus)
3) We will reward with a treat for acceptable behavior (Positive Motivation)

To initiate the dog to sit, we simply use the dog's favorite toy, treat, a hot dog, etc. and tell the dog the "Sit" command as we slowly move the treat beyond the dog's snout, just over their head. As the dog attempts to follow, it will usually place its rear on the ground, which is a sit.

At the moment its rear is on the ground, we give the dog a strong, happy "Good Boy" or "Good Girl," followed by a treat. It is important that the treat follow the praise because the praise is what the dog is, and primarily will be, working for. The treat is a positive reinforcement that strengthens the positive association with performing this activity in response to the given stimulus.

As we continue through this process a few times, the dog will become more and more prepared and eager to sit for us, even beginning to perform the act before being given the command, in anticipation of the reward.

After polishing this event, we can analyze the process with exactly how it lines up with our theory. The sit position has become our Conditioned Response (1), the "Sit" command has become our Stimulus (2), and the treat, along with praise, has been used as the Positive Motivation for reproducing this activity (3).

Though this is a generic, even elementary example, this is how ALL conditioning takes place, whether it be good or bad, whether we realize it or not, and regardless of whether engaging the process is intentional or inadvertent.

In an alternate example, we can clearly show how the use of force and compulsion in the process will produce grossly different final results.

We give the dog the "Sit" command. When he does not comply, the handler stiffly pulls upwards on the leash, tightening a chain around the dog's neck, causing pain and discomfort. This can be with a regular choke chain or with a prong collar. Electricity can also be substituted in this scenario, but instead of pulling the leash, the button would be pressed on the transmitter, initiating a shock to the dog's neck. The idea is to cause pain.

At this point, it is important to understand a major flaw in this process. Since this is the first exposure of the dog to performing the sit in response to our command, is obviously a learning event. If this is so, then why would it be appropriate for the handler to apply correction to the dog for failing to obey? This is grossly unfair. The dog has absolutely no idea at this point what constitutes obedience.

After numerous evolutions, the dog finally sits, or the chain and leash may be used to physically attempt to place him in position; he then may get a "Good Boy." Many repetitions later, the dog may begin to sit readily.

After looking into this second scenario, we can analyze the process and determine exactly how the above process applies. Initially, one would perceive that the sit position has become the Conditioned Response (1), the "Sit" command has become the Stimulus (2), and application of the chain/electricity has been used as the Negative Motivation in response to the dog not producing the desire activity (3).

Conversely, this is wrong. Though the position of the dog in a sit has become our Conditioned Response (1), and the command "Sit" is used, "Fear of Reprisal" has become our Stimulus (2), combined with a confusion caused from the use of both Positive and Negative Motivation (3) within the same event. Since the chain is always there, though not always restrictive or choking, we have taken away the dog's opportunity to think through problems and to make decisions. The dog now will often begin to dread the leash and collar, and most working scenarios associated with their use.

This is also a dog that now operates not in drive, exhibiting an eagerness to please, but out of fear of reprisal. He attempts to perform a task not because it is beneficial or enjoyable to him, but to escape pain and punishment. Then we praise him for this behavior with the "Good Boy" when he finally exhibits a behavior or activity we think we understand (the sitting position).

The dog is rewarded (3-Positive/Negative Motivation) for exhibiting an action out of fear (1-Conditioned Response) initiated by repeated pain given by the handler (2-Stimulus).

If we return to the first scenario, there is absolutely zero possibility of destroying drive or creating a fear of reprisal. The act of correction in this scenario simply does not exist. However, if the dog does not perform our desired tasks, we simply withhold the reward. He then learns that in order to bring this reward about faster, he must exhibit the desired behavior (that which has been previously rewarded) in a much quicker manner. This is a dog working in drive, and will exhibit reliable, reproducible results without the handler being dependent on various devices to create the element of fear within the dog while working.

Understanding these simple principles will benefit use in every facet of working with the dog. We demonstrate these principles in all aspects of our involvement with the dog on a day-to-day basis.

Chapter Nine

Rolodex Theory

As complex as the dog may first seem, they actually view their world quite simply. Not possessing the capacity to run long lines of reasoning, the dog digests each situation, environment or scenario and reacts to each one based its most closely related previous experience.

The purpose of this chapter is to give a simplified, brief overview of how the dog stores these experiences, processes the information, and subsequently renders an action or reaction in response.

Most everyone is familiar with a Rolodex, the card filing device used to alphabetically organize personal and business information. This is the simplest, most tangible example of how efficiently and directly the dog's mind processes information.

In the Rolodex, the cards are divided into individual sections. On the top of the first card for each section is a tab containing one letter of the alphabet, sequential from the first, categorizing the sections alphabetically. Within each section, the cards of information are further organized based upon their alphabetical relationship to other cards within the section.

To understand this analogy more fully, we will incorporate the Pavlovian Theory discussed earlier. Simply put, the lettered tabs will be considered the Stimulus, the information contained or "written" on the card in regards to the action or reaction to the Stimulus is the Conditioned Response.

There is also additional information contained within a particular card. Not only is the specific stimulus found there, but the card also contains information regarding the dog's past actions, behaviors or activities he exhibited in response to previous exposures to the stimulus.

Finally, the card contains information based upon previous responses of whether the outcome is viewed as positive or negative for the dog. This information determines if the past activity or behavior was rewarded or punished.

To begin to put this analogy in place with practical application, we will discuss the simple obedience exercise of the sit. The spoken command "Sit" would obviously be the stimulus to bring about this activity from the dog. At this spoken command by the handler, in a fraction of a second, the relevant card pops up for the dog to "read." This example shows not only how simple this process is, but also how important the correct imprinting process is.

If imprinted correctly, the dog will understand from the information gathered and stored during previous experiences with this stimulus that he is expected to assume a sitting posture.

Before any change in activity or posture takes place, the dog will also evaluate the previous outcomes of this event, based upon his activity or behavior exhibited in past responses to the stimulus. If this activity or behavior has brought about praise or reward in a consistent manner, the dog will then be quick to exhibit the behavior, activity, or posture. If the activity or behavior has brought about negative reinforcement through means for correction, or even the withholding of the reward, the dog will be slower to exhibit this activity, and ultimately will not exhibit such activity or behavior at all.

If the dog has been exposed to confusing outcomes for a particular stimulus (sometimes there was praise or reward associated with the activity or behavior, while at other times, there was negative reinforcement or correction for the same activity or behavior), the dog then experiences a great deal of conflict. Presented with this particular conflicting "card," the dog will be very reluctant to act. Because of this conflicting information, the dog is unsure whether the exhibition of the activity or behavior for this particular stimulus will be rewarded or punished by the handler. As a result, the handler will see either no change in activity or behavior, or the dog will exhibit a completely different activity or behavior than desired. This is an attempt by the dog to avoid correction while searching for appropriate and rewarded behavior.

The handler must also understand that if a "bad" or conflicting card exists, unlike the real Rolodex, it can never be removed. These conflicting and often confusing cards will accompany the dog throughout its life. This permanent attachment of the cards to the dog means we have to be very careful how they are handled. Most importantly, as a handler, we want to ensure as best as we possibly can that these bad or conflicting cards are not being acknowledged or constantly brought back up for the dog.

Since we can never remove these bad or conflicting cards, we can never be absolutely sure they will never be raised by some outside influence or stimulus. This is especially true when we do not know a dog's history. Without a solid knowledge of the dog's history, what they have or have not been exposed to, what negative stimuli or conflicting cards may exist and so on, we can never be 100% certain what activities may elicit undesirable behavior.

What we can do for such dogs is create as much positive training evolution as possible, while at the same time, exposing the dog to as many external stimuli as possible: environments, working evolutions, adults, children, other dogs, etc. This provides two benefits for us.

First, if through the exposure to a particular stimulus, it becomes obvious the dog has either no association or has a positive association with the stimulus, then this exposure has now turned into a positive training evolution. This builds the dog's confidence, while strengthening the dog and handler bond.

Second, if the dog exhibits a bad or conflicting association with this particular stimulus, we must then work to suppress these bad or conflicting cards as much as possible. At the same time, we must also be conscious that this particular stimulus may bring about undesirable or unpredictable behavior in the future.

Since we cannot remove these conflicting cards, we must consider the only approach left for dealing with them. As trainers and handlers, we are charged with creating a new, more attractive card for this particular stimulus. For basic obedience, this is easily addressed by simply changing the stimulus. For example, instead of English, work the dog with commands in another language.

Since there is no association with the new commands, the dog can put together the related activities rather quickly, but without the confusion and conflict. This change, however, once made must be committed to. If a language change for this example is made, then we cannot continue to expose the dog to the old stimulus, or the commands in English. For conflicting cards concerning stimulus, we must then work to create positive training evolutions where the dog is exposed to the stimulus but in a new, positive manner. By continuing to do so, the card for this particular stimulus will be outweighed with positives over any negative present.

By understanding this process, we can begin to understand many issues that a particular dog may have. Early imprinting on the dog (or lack thereof), will set the stage for a great amount of the dog's abilities and character throughout its life. Training and conditioning regimens that are conflicting and confusing for the dog will create problems throughout the dog's life when relevant stimuli are present.

Conversely, if we create as many positive training events and evolutions possible, we are set to build, by influence, an animal that will exhibit high confidence and character. This dog will learn readily and engage new stimuli in a manner that allows the conditioning process to be taken on with positive outcomes. This dog will neither be fearful nor overly aggressive, as it does not feel threatened by new environments, situations, or scenarios. This dog has a strong history of events it has encountered in a positive light, and from this history is eager to engage new environments, situations, or scenarios.

Chapter Ten

Choke Chains, Pinch Collars, and Electricity

It has become commonplace in many circles of the current dog industry to utilize force and compulsion by way of choke chains, the pinch or prong collar, and electric collars. Typically, these are not only recommended by a majority of veterinarians, but also by most training facilities throughout the country.

You can walk into almost any dog facility of any sort and find these devices openly displayed and subsequently recommended to you because they are believed to be essential in order to teach your dog to heel, sit, down, etc. The key word I use here is "essential."

There are many trainers that can put a dog on a prong and shock collar and get the dog to perform the desired task, most of them yanking the prong and shocking the dog as they give the command. There are many handlers who work their dogs with these devices, again applying the correction with the command. The same is true for pet owners. The command "Sit" is applied at the same the yank or shock is applied. This is incorrect training folks. Many people are purchasing dogs along with a quick handler course on the correct way to handle their dogs and that is what they are taught. I am sorry, but in my world, if you purchase a fully trained dog and you have to work your dog on a prong or shock collar, your dog is not finished training.

Most of these devices were originally meant to be used by trainers in the industry dealing with hard dogs, and solve specific behavioral issues, *not* for every dog to be trained with them all the time. We have too many loose cannons running around with these devices and there are way too many dogs in society that are dependent upon them in order to work, which does nothing but create more liability. The best trainers I have found in this industry do not pull out the metal in order to condition a dog at first sight; unfortunately they are few and far between.

Advocates of these poor training practices simply do not truly understand the correct process in its entirety. They are taught that the use of these devices brings about the desired result(s) with the dog quickly. Let's say that what they believe was actually true, that by using this type of force and compulsion, one obtains the desired result(s) quicker. Still, what most of these advocates do not realize is that with all the yanking of the chain or pinch collar, and shocking from the electric collar, the dog actually begins to work out of fear of reprisal.

Possibly, some people have made the decision to use these devices because they feel the presence of all this hardware makes them (not necessarily the dog) look good, official, or important, thereby not exhibiting the trait of being "even." You know, the "my dog has to wear this because he is so tough," or because he is so unruly. There are those who say "my dog can't be trusted," or "my dog is handler aggressive." It is common for those who choose to use these devices to end up with dogs that are ultimately either overly submissive and confused, or unpredictable and calloused.

What exactly are we exhibiting to the dog by utilizing such tools of force and compulsion? To truly grasp the premise of this chapter, we must first understand that the dog is a pack animal, one dependent upon others within the pack. We must also understand how the hierarchy of the pack dictates desired or undesired behavior.

It is important to note that at no time will one canine aggressively raise a paw or front leg to strike another, even during an exhibition of juvenile fighting. (This is not to be confused with the dog's placement of his forelegs upon an adversary to steady himself during a fight, or as an attempt to push away an aggressor when rolled on his back.) This raising of the paw will be exhibited, regardless of age, by the canine in such manner to initiate play or interaction, to continue the current game, or to initiate a new one. This is an activity of social interaction. We imitate this activity when we pet the dog; an exhibition on our part of approval of the dog's performance or obedience, or consolation of the dog while expressing our affection for him.

We must also understand that the canine, though possessing a limited ability to reason, cannot run long lines of reasoning. Since a raised paw is never interpreted as an aggressive nor corrective measure within the pack setting, and the dog has come to know us and our families as the adjusted pack, the canine simply cannot truly comprehend the idea of being struck by us. It is simply not an integral activity within the canine societal structure. Striking your dog as a form of correction will only cause the dog to work out of its fear of reprisal, instead of confidence.

Remember, as the handler, you are responsible for establishing effective communication on the dog's level. Striking with your hand (or an object in your hand) is not a corrective measure in any language your dog understands.

While some may believe that striking the dog with either an open or closed hand is corrective in nature to the dog, our act of hitting the dog actually creates an environment of confusion and conflict. In the canine's perception, he has just experienced a violent act, one that has brought pain upon his body, and the handler has caused this pain. However, he cannot truly make the correlation of corrective action as we perceive it, since this is not a natural activity or mannerism within the pack environment. The dog may eventually begin to cower. Though this may be the desired result of the handler, the cowering posture arises primarily out of the dog's confusion. He is confused by the pain he is experiencing, stemming from an activity that is supposed to be pleasing (petting with the hand). He also experiences conflict over why the handler (Alpha) has taken the number one, most meaningful reward, and turned it against him.

Now that we understand why the dog cannot understand being struck as a form of correction, let's add additional tools of force and compulsion.

If one were to place a corrective device upon a person, such as a choke-chain or pinch-collar, we would quickly rush to classify this as cruel and inhumane treatment. The victim of this treatment would understand and comprehend not only who placed the device on him, but also why. This person also understands the subsequent corrective measures which may ensue should he exhibit undesired behavior, even though he may be unaware at the time of what those undesired behaviors may be. He quickly becomes acutely aware that he has absolutely no physical control over the device, whether or not it will be used, or to what extent. However, he does begin to grasp an understanding of desirable behavior and frequency with which he should exhibit it—at least as defined by the human being in control of the pain-inflicting device.

Once such devices are actually employed, the recipient clearly understands the corrective measures as a result of many factors. Most notably; human beings are pugilistic by nature, a species which engages in corrective measures and/or combat by the use of their limbs in an effort to apply force and/or pain to either an adversary or subordinate in order to effect a change in the subject's behavior. From this, we understand correction and aggression stemming from the use of the hand(s) of another, as well as aggressively confronting an adversary by the use of our hands is a trait and behavior we as humans exhibit, not the dog. We accept this activity as part of our genetic make-up. Every human being will exhibit it to one extent or another.

Due to our expanded abilities to run longer lines of reasoning, we can also associate the previously discussed devices with an extension of the hand, that is, to extend the ability to apply force or pain at extended distances.

At no point during the development or evolution of the *Canis Familiaris* species has one canine used such tools or tactics upon another. This is fact, simply because the dog possesses neither an appreciation nor understanding of aggressive or corrective striking using the forelimbs. Nor does it understand devices such as choke chains, pinch collars, or electrical devices, nor can there be any true, complete understanding or comprehension of the utilization of such. Without this understanding and comprehension of these methods or devices, the canine cannot begin to comprehend the implementation of such, specifically when such implementation results in conflict and confusion, further preventing the dog from exhibiting the natural traits, drives and characteristics for which they were originally bred.

I would much rather have a dog work with me out of confidence and trust derived from clear, concise communication on a level that we both understand, than a dog that will only work for me when these devices are used, simply because he has been conditioned to work out of fear of reprisal. I have dealt with numerous handlers who, once they have received the proper education, actually become quite angry at how society not only accepts these devices, but teaches that use of these devices towards the dog is actually acceptable behavior. I have seen many grown men and women shed a tear and go apologize to their dog, now considered their partner, for having exhibited such behavior and utilized such devices. This is a situation where the relationship really begins to emerge into a team.

Chapter Eleven

Understanding the Shelter Dog

The dog lives to please us, yet most spend their lives being misunderstood and disrespected, as has been covered in previous chapters. This misunderstanding and disrespect are the very reasons so many dogs ultimately end up in shelters or rescue environments. Others are poor education, or a lack of responsibility, care and/or concern for dogs, as is often exhibited by individuals or families that decide to purchase a puppy or dog, yet are unwilling to research the breed (or breeds, if mixed) before the purchase. These individuals do not accept the core responsibilities of owning a pet, such as providing appropriate exercise, housebreaking, respect for the dog as an integral member of the family, and establishing acceptable perimeters through giving proper directions.

Dogs are also left behind by loved ones who have passed on, by owners who surrender them due to health problems, or through displacement due to natural disasters. Wouldn't it be nice if shelter organizations would focus more time, effort and money on outreach programs for those who find themselves in such a predicament? Instead, they focus on taking care of the unwanted and uncared for dogs. Imagine for just one minute how it would be if none of these organizations existed.

Sadly, some dogs simply should never have been born. In particular, there are dogs that exist merely as a result of those I label "backyard breeders." You know the ones. They carelessly breed their dog to a friend or neighbor's dog simply because they look similar to a particular breed, giving little to no consideration to the traits and characteristics essential to the makeup of the particular breeds involved.

Worse than the backyard breeders, there are those that allow intact males and females to just do their thing at will in the backyard, freely roaming and breeding throughout the neighborhood and streets of our society. This is incredibly irresponsible. These people behave as if they have no idea dogs do things like this twice a year. This often results in puppies being whelped under abandoned and unoccupied homes, schoolyards, or even culverts in our parks.

Some of these dogs also come from puppy mills and hoarders. Even more tragic is that we now have individual fosters and rescue groups committing the same negligence.

Then there are those dogs that come from other abusive and neglectful environments. The ones who are rescued after having been left behind or abused, like those tethered by a rope, collar or chain that has grown into the skin of their neck. There are the ones who have been left to roam and survive on their own. There are those who come from a home of violence, where they have been struck, kicked, or even stabbed, as well as the ones who come in with heartworms due to irresponsibility of their handlers in providing preventative care. Still others have been tethered to trees or chain link fencing on three-foot ropes, standing in their feces, remaining alive after witnessing the death of their littermates who were hung from their tethers. These are those who are emaciated and/or beaten into pitifully frail state of being. A life of emptiness and fear is all they know. These dogs each carry a Rolodex full of cards that simply are not fair, and we are the ones to blame—not the dog. Yet it is the dog who suffers...is it not?

There are also dogs that come from the fight ring. Bait dogs that are tied to trees with logging chains around their neck, with barbed wire around their muzzle and through their mouth. Dogs kept isolated in damp, dark basements. Dogs that have been ripped apart while fighting that draw their last breath of air in your arms. Just as there are those who come from the fight ring, there are those who come from the bait ring. Dogs who have been beaten down, having had their legs broken with baseball bats, and been left defenseless, laying around in the yard, their teeth filed or pulled to eliminate any possibility of defense in order to serve as a training aid to their fighting dogs.

When dealing with dogs as mentioned above, it is imperative to understand the cards that may be present, whether they be good or bad, but it is just as important to understand how to deal with them on a level the dog can understand. I hope this chapter will be some guidance or assistance to those who operate within this industry.

Specifically, when dealing with litters of puppies, one must understand pack structure. On occasion, in professional breeding facilities and shelter environments I have observed a dominant littermate pick on a weaker member. It is the one who is the weakest; the one who is getting picked on that often gets removed from the littler, coddled and petted. By removing the weaker puppy from the litter; they are pitied, and this is wrong.

The proper way to handle a situation such as this is to remove the overly dominant pup form the litter when it exhibits this behavior; however, the puppy should not be removed and then reprimanded for the behavior previously exhibited within the litter. He needs to simply be removed to a crate or kennel and not one word needs to be spoken to him. I would leave him there until I knew, through his behavior, that he had processed exactly what had taken place.

Given this situation in a completely primal pack structure, the Beta would correct or punish the overly dominate one, not the more submissive one. In many cases, I have witnessed beta's put a youngster in their place and make them stay there until the slate was clean.

Each member not only needs, but wants the interaction from the pack. Separation from the pack is a form of punishment for antisocial behavior. The young dog rapidly learns that in order to be allowed further interaction within the pack, he must conduct himself accordingly. This separation time could include interaction with a complementary littermate, or even spending time playing games, focusing energy in a positive way. The age of the puppy will dictate the amount of time the separation should last, whether it is for a few minutes, a few hours throughout the day, or possibly even longer at times. However, he must not be permanently removed from the pack at this age, as this would do far more damage than good to the young dog.

When raising a litter, it is imperative to understand that we cannot dictate pack order, but must allow this to be worked out between each the litter members, assisting them only when absolutely necessary. We must always remember that what is primal to us may not be so primal to the dog. Sometimes dogs are coddled and petted way too much when they need to simply step it up.

There are many issues that arise when working with dogs that come from an abusive or neglectful environment. For example, shelter employees will often mistakenly label a dog as having "food aggression" because the dog is protective of its meal. Some communities go so far as to have a "good dog" certification wherein the dog is expected to remain passive towards other encroaching dogs while eating and even allow someone to pet the dog's face or place one's hand *in the bowl* while the dog is eating! While we have had many generations to "dummy down" some of the canine instincts, protecting a meal isn't one we are likely to remove during the reign of man, nor should we ever try.

Such "man-ufactured" requirements are not only wrong, but hugely disrespectful to the dog. Again, this is not behavior that is exhibited within the canine pack structure, so one must ask why we accept it. Imagine you had to depend upon someone for your food and someone else took it away from you. How would you feel? Think about this, because the key word here is DEPEND.

In the pack setting, a dog will be directed by the alpha or beta as to when it is appropriate for them to eat because they have *earned* the right to eat. Then, it will stand its ground to defend or fight for his food, or wait for what is left. A true

Alpha or Beta will not express to another dog that it is his time to eat, and then take the food away from him. When your dog is fed, he accepts that he has earned that food and therefore has the right to protect it. These are primal cards in his Rolodex and they cannot be removed. To attempt to do so is to try to remove elements that truly define the species. A dog that most would call "food aggressive," to me is typically a dog that is a survivor, warrior and conqueror. These "food aggressive" actions may be an exhibition of drive, will, commitment, and even an element of respect. However, this may also show me insecurity, and continued episodes of challenging this dog for his food will only prove to increase this insecurity.

I have been to shelters, rescues and other such establishments and observed dogs that had previously been starved and abused being not only kept in the same pen together, but fed in the same pen as well. These dogs need to be fed in private. They need to feel that there is no threat of their food being taken from them. They need to understand that his food comes from you, and it is a gift.

In order to be fair to the dog, we must not set him up to be challenged by making him fear his food will be taken away. The dog needs to grow not only physically, but mentally as well. They need to be communicated with on this level so they can understand and be given an opportunity to learn to trust. Therefore, new cards must be created. In order to completely stand with the dog, when encountering situations such as this, one must also be prepared to help the dog learn to stand.

I have worked with many dogs that have experienced such turmoil, dogs that were so hungry and frightened that they exhibited many different forms of aggression. They would snarl and bare their teeth out of fear while running to hide at the back of their kennel or yard—much of this with just cause.

When working with dogs that have these cards, one has to exhibit all of the prerequisites required to both understand and exhibit the five responsibilities of Alpha. One has to understand and apply the three ways to deal with a dog in an effort to become a team.

Upon the seizure or surrender of a dog to a shelter facility, the dog will typically need at least three days to adjust to its new environment. If the dog needs to endure a stay at a veterinarian clinic due to illness and/or injury, then more time will most likely be needed.

During the three day acclimation period, do not try to force a relationship upon the dog. Allow the dog space and time to evaluate the new environment, the people involved, and the day-to-day activities to which he is being exposed. Enter their environment only to provide food, water, and the opportunity for the dog to empty, if kept in a concrete kennel or crate. First and foremost, remember, everything a dog does is based upon previous experience, or lack thereof.

Spend time sitting in front of his or her kennel or crate during these first few days with your back turned, never once turning to face him. Do not acknowledge any submissive or aggressive behavior of any kind. By having our back turned to the dog in a situation such as this, regardless of the behavior he or she may exhibit, we are exposing the dog to strength, courage, and trust with zero possibility of the dog misinterpreting our actions as those of aggression, threat, or violence. During this time, read a book, preferably this one (to continue to stamp your cards that have been created), and basically, ignore the dog.

You may witness wetting, extreme salivation, muscle twitching, or that the dog is physically shaking, as if wet. This shaking, which we call the stress shake, stems from confusion, conflict, anxiety, and stress within the dog. In extreme cases, the dog may even release his bowels.

During these three days, allow the dog to see positive interaction between dog and human, without removing him or her from the safety and security of the kennel or crate. Be sure to allow the dog to witness you feeding another dog pieces of hot dog from your hand in reward for acceptable and desired behavior. (I feel this is also important when dealing with submissive or aggressive type behavior of most any kind.)

On the fourth day, you can typically approach the kennel and begin the process of rehabilitation and conditioning. This is a long and enduring process of creating new cards and stamping them appropriately, while understanding that we can never erase the dog's old cards.

With hot dog in hand (and pocket), approach the kennel and sit with your back turned as usual. First, wait to see if the dog will approach you and what behavior he exhibits. He will then choose to accept you by either sniffing or nudging you through the enclosure, then returning to the position of safety toward the back. The most favorable situation would be that he or she chooses to sit or even lay down behind you. If the dog chooses to approach you and begins to sniff or nudge you, slowly and carefully slip a small piece of hot dog into the enclosure. Do this just a couple of times, then get up and leave the dog. You can choose to visit the dog again on that same day, but I recommend no more than three times. Always follow the same procedure as you did in the first visit.

On the following day, begin with your back turned, and after the first piece of hot dog has been given, begin to make a quarter turn to either side, being parallel to the dog. At this point, the dog may turn away. Remain in your position and wait patiently. Do not call to or try to coax the dog to you, yet raise your head occasionally to take a look. You could toss a small piece of hot dog into the enclosure occasionally. If the dog takes the hot dog, then calmly, in a soft but firm tone tell him or her, "Good Dog."

In time, depending on the circumstances and the case, the dog will begin to grow both physically and mentally. If this is a dog that has come from abuse and neglect, you will most likely witness the dog begin to exhibit strong commitment to the handler or animal caretaker. Be very careful with this, especially if your goal is to eventually place this dog in an adoptive environment. These dogs sometimes over-compensate with their love, adoration, and affection, and may even exhibit some behaviors towards others that might be mistakenly interpreted as aggressive or even vicious. Keeping this in mind, it is very crucial that once the dog indicates he has gained a level of confidence (perhaps by happily wagging his tail while waiting to be interacted with), that we begin introducing him to new environments and new people.

When introducing new people, it is important to follow this initial conditioning phase of the particular dog. The first introduction should consist of the original handler and another person who has been properly educated in how to deal with such dogs. This person should begin interacting with the dog by kneeling down on the dog's level, gaining his or her trust even through the kennel or crate. The original handler should remain standing, only kneeling down on the dog's level periodically. This too represents courage, strength, and trust.

Hopefully, in time, the dog will indicate to you when he or she is ready to encounter and engage new challenges. Allow the dog to communicate to you on a level he or she can, and do your best to understand this effort at communication. This also means understanding that no matter how many good cards we may create, we cannot guarantee the bad cards will never rear their ugly head again. Remember, as sad as this is, once the card is created, it will always be there. This is not like removing a hard drive from a computer and being able to erase it. These bad or damaged cards will always exist.

Understanding that we are working with the dog and not against him, we expose him to new people and/or environments when it is appropriate. Through time and experience, you will learn when to prolong a certain exposure or event, or when the dog just needs to cowboy or cowgirl up and do it. There does, however, need to be the realization of when there are just too many bad cards stacked against a particular dog. Sometimes, euthanasia is truly the only humane choice left for a dog.

When one takes on the responsibility of operating a rescue or shelter facility, it is imperative that it be done fairly, and be conducted on a level and in such manner the dog can understand. It is no better for a dog that has been starved and tethered to be put in a kennel and not experience the outdoors for days. Nor is it fair for the dog to be kenneled outside and denied the social interaction he desires and needs on a daily basis.

The main goal of any shelter or rescue facility is to find permanent homes for the dog where he or she will be taken in as an integral part of the family. A permanent home where the dog will feel he or she will feel safe, and have a purpose within the pack. The remainder of this chapter will focus on topics suggested by various shelter and foster groups throughout our country.

Utilizing the Crate

There are those who feel the crate is a bad thing, or that it is inhumane to crate a dog. Their fears and concerns are unfounded. Crating has many benefits when used properly.

Crate training is a course of action that needs to be implemented during the conditioning process. It will ultimately benefit the dog by creating habits that will increase the adoptability of the dog through ease of integration within the adoptive home. When individuals come to us for training, we recommend they bring a crate for their dog, or we will use one we have. This allows the dog a safe place to rest and recuperate, especially if more than one dog will be out training. It also allows him the opportunity to think about and process the event(s) in which he or she has just participated.

The crate, when used properly, provides the dog with a sense of security, solace and privacy. It allows the dog to be in a safe place that resembles a den. Because of this, we do not recommend the open wire collapsible crates. These are not only potentially unsafe for the dog, but provide no sense of security or privacy for the dog. Our preference is a crate with more solid sides, especially on the bottom half, while still allowing for adequate ventilation.

In addition, if the dog is placed in a properly sized crate, the process of housebreaking the dog will move much more smoothly. The size of the crate is important because if a dog, especially a very young dog, is placed in too large of a crate, it will be much more apt to relieve itself while inside the crate. A properly sized crate allows the dog to stand, turn around and lie down comfortably. It is also worth noting that when a dog is fed in his crate, he has no fear or threat of challenge over his food.

Crates also provide the dog with firm structure. For example, when one takes on a dog that has co-dependency issues or separation anxiety, a crate is a great tool to assist in building the confidence of that particular dog. It creates both an environment and opportunity for the dog to learn to become comfortable when left alone. Typically, a dog that is fearful of the crate is fearful out of the crate as well.

Fence Climbers

Even the best natured dogs can easily find themselves labeled as the dreaded "fence climber." Though there are actually few reasons for dogs to climb fences, fence climbers are typically seeking acceptance, approval, and interaction. The fence climber has become overwhelmed by stimulation on the outside of the fence, whether it is another dog, a small animal, or a female in heat that he can smell and seeks to find. The exhibition of this behavior, though there are always exceptions to the rule, is most often a by-product of neglect on the part of the handler. If the dog is not receiving necessary interaction and acceptance from us (the other member(s) of his pack), then he will often resort to creating his own outlet for them. Interactions and acceptance are essential components of pack structure.

Once a dog successfully climbs over a fence, we will be hard pressed to circumvent further efforts of climbing. This dog has discovered that by crossing to the other side of the fence, he can engage in many elements of self-gratification, while experiencing many new activities on his own. The very act of climbing the fence to the other side has become a self-rewarding activity for the dog.

There are many suggestions for addressing the fence climber, but most importantly, there must be an immediate increase in the interaction between the owner and the dog and the dog must not be left outside unsupervised. Both of these go a long way in decreasing the attractiveness of the stimulation outside the fence. For the dog that must remain outside, no-climb fences (ones where the tops actually turn inward), are very effective.

While we do always recommend a fenced yard for turning the dog out, we do not recommend underground electric fences.

The underground fences provide an electrical shock to the dog via a receiver collar fitted to the dog. Once the dog approaches a predetermined distance from the buried wire, the collar receives a radio signal that triggers the electrical shock. The premise of these systems is that the dog quickly learns how far out in the yard it can travel, while avoiding the shock, in turn establishing the boundaries in which the dog is allowed to operate. The reality of this process carries some glaring flaws.

First, this buried wire only affects the wearer of the receiver collar. These types of boundary systems have absolutely no affect on any other animal; therefore cannot prevent any intrusion. Any other dog can come into the yard and start fights or breed the contained dog, and any other animal, wild or domestic, can enter into the dog's defined area.

Secondly, if a dog is contained within such a system and wearing the appropriate receiver collar, but exceeds the bounds of the system, he will be prevented from getting back into his own area. For example, if the dog begins to give chase to a small animal, the energy rush of the prey drive, coupled with high speed, may well prevent him from acknowledging the electrical shock. His speed simply carries him beyond the bounds of the radio receiver.

Once on the outside, after the chase is over, the dog is prevented from returning home, for when he reaches the proximity of the buried wire, he receives the same shock as he would by approaching the buried wire from the inside. Since he is no longer in an elevated level of prey drive and is no longer moving fast, he will not be able to endure the electrical shock, and will distance himself from any area in which he receives the shock.

The Catchpole

Though a useful and often necessary tool, the catchpole is misused way too often in the animal industry. When time will not allow for an ingested tranquilizer to take effect, it is typically appropriate to tranquilize the dog by use of the dart gun. Bear in mind that the catchpole is inherently a violent device in the dog's eyes, although it can be used without injury to the animal. It is a device in a person's hand that restricts the dog's movement, inspires fight or flight responses and may restrict airflow and cause panic in the dog. Those are not experiences we want an "even" dog to endure. This is not to say they should never be used, however, I contend there are better "first resort" tactics.

Many animal professionals involved in shelter and rescue organizations are often quick to grab the catchpole simply because a dog is of a particular breed. Some organizations actually have policies in place that dictate this exact protocol. Sometimes, however, the human at the end of the catchpole is of uneven character and has a need to feel in control, and takes no time to even try to understand the dog at all.

Another misuse of the catchpole is on injured dogs, when the user does not correctly interpret the attitude or behavior exhibited by the dog. The use of the catchpole in these circumstances may well aggravate the injury sustained by the dog, creating further adverse behavior, either evasive or aggressive in nature.

The dog on the catchpole cannot understand the constriction around its neck, coupled with the sudden limitation of its mobility. Once these two factors are in place, the dog's primal reaction is fight or flight, just as with all other animals. If the dog has been injured, (whether before or after introduction of the catchpole), this primal reaction will be multiplied. From the dog's point of view, this device has increased it pain and restricted its movement—and the next step will be its ultimate demise.

Am I saying we need to do away with all catchpoles? Absolutely not. There are justifiable uses for the catchpole, specifically when injury to people in the immediate environment is eminent and there is no opportunity for tranquilization. However, even in these circumstances, the catchpole should be used while maintaining a strong concern for the dog's well-being. Every attempt should be made to de-escalate the level of violence, to avoid causing any further injury or trauma to the dog by use of the pole. Also, the pole should be used no longer than absolutely necessary.

We must be extremely cautious of using the catchpole too hastily. We must not use it merely because we may not understand a particular dog, are frightened of its breed, or cannot accurately interpret the behavior exhibited by the dog. Remember, this is an uncomfortable situation for the dog too.

Timidity

Timidity is easiest described as dogs exhibiting a fear of any social interaction. Timid dogs are typically fearful of new environments, people or dogs. They will often exhibit wetting and may become quite reclusive. These dogs may also be in poor physical condition or even close to emaciation because they have been housed with other much stronger dogs, and will not compete for food. Severe cases of timidity will not even accept food when offered from a person. These will often not seek any interaction at all with people, and will be extremely difficult to approach. They cannot be petted.

Timidity stems from poor or lacking socialization during the first windows of a dog's life. As discussed before, the period between six and fourteen weeks of age is the most impressionable and important time of a dog's life. It is during that time that the stage is set for a large portion of the dog's personality, temperament, and disposition.

If the dog is removed from the litter too early during this window of time, he will not learn to interact within acceptable parameters, thus the skill sets necessary for successful social interaction will not be created. The dog does not learn to play, to develop fighting and defensive skills, or the value of praise, acceptance and correction.

Since it is common for puppies to be removed from the litter early on during this window, to be sold or given away (typically between six and eight weeks of age), most of these dogs will arrive at a new home where these skill sets will neither be developed nor promoted. The owner, more often than not, does not have solid information and education in regard to the dog. The typical owner knows nothing of pack structure nor the imprinting the dog requires to mature into a well-balanced, even-tempered, properly socialized adult. The dog is left to its own devices to develop and establish operational parameters.

If we wish to effectively deal with the timid dog, we must begin by first gaining his trust. This process will not be immediate, and may even be quite lengthy. It is imperative that we do not pursue the dog. We must not attempt to force a relationship with the dog, for this pressure will only increase his timidity. This trust may be developed over time by the use of food reward and positive motivation to build the dog's character. However, the absolute first step is one the dog must take. He must begin to accept us on his own.

This acceptance begins by the dog choosing to approach the handler. This may be very slow at first. He may only get close enough to the handler to investigate. Again, it is imperative that no attempt be made at this point to touch the dog. If enough time is allowed (and this may take a number of sessions with the dog), the dog will dictate when it is prepared for further contact. Only when the dog expresses this desire for further interaction should the next step be taken in this process.

The next step is to actually touch the dog. This touching should be done from kneeling or crouching position, but not by leaning over the dog, for this could be interpreted by him as aggressive or authoritative posturing. The attempt to touch or pat the dog should be slow and deliberate; preferably by rubbing the dog on the underside of the neck and or by small pats on the chest. Because the handler will most likely not know the entire history of the dog, it is extremely important that he or she not attempt to pat the dog on top of the head. Nor should the handler make large or exaggerated gestures over the dog with his or her arms, as these actions may serve as a catalyst for the timid nature (if the dog suffers from prior abuse).

Over time, if we are consistent in our communication to the dog that we mean no harm, pose no threat, and have no intention to abuse him, the dog will most likely begin to develop more and more trust of us.

There are, however, absolutely zero guarantees that this dog will ever reach a level of character that will allow him to function and interact on the level one would consider typical for the given breed. The dog may not even choose to interact with a person, even with the influence of food. Because this dog has been prevented from developing the skill set necessary for social interaction during that early window of time in his life, he may simply lack the foundation on which solid character is built. As sad as this may be, remember this stems solely from poor breeding, care and rearing of the dog.

The Overcompensating Dog

The overcompensating dog is actually quite similar to the dog exhibiting a timid disposition, as each of these dispositions stem from fear created out of a lack of socialization and proper imprinting as a puppy.

Instead of a timid nature, this type of dog has taken the position that he must make everyone believe he is the greatest threat and the most dominant of adversaries. Essentially, this dog bluffs his way through life. Just as the schoolyard bully, this dog believes that by appearing to be the greater adversary, he can ward off any threat by an exhibition of aggression or violence. Conversely, this dog rarely has the foundation to back up this facade if he actually ever were to be challenged.

This dog often aggressively engages smaller or weaker opponents, and will often exhibit an unwarranted violent behavior towards passive, non-threatening people and animals. He believes that as long as he can continue to portray himself in this manner, he will never actually have to face any opponent. He believes he can ward off any opponent before escalation begins.

The overcompensating dog may be worked with, and may also appear to progress in his social skill set to a point where positive interaction with other dogs is possible. Still, this is not quickly corrected, and must be addressed by the slow introduction of the dog to other stable, well socialized animals. However, just as with other conditions stemming from poor imprinting during the early stage, the dog may never truly overcome the condition to the point that he can be considered trustworthy around other dogs.

At the opposite end of the spectrum, sometimes the shelter or rescue dog will overcompensate by exhibiting behavior such as excessive jumping and constant licking. The dog is showing affection, happiness, love and is very thankful, but he is beyond excessive with it. This behavior is very primal. The dog is overcompensating. This could be because the dog is so thankful to have been rescued and is now part of a pack. Or it could be that the dog lacks social interaction or behavior training. Excessive licking can also stem from a traumatic experience in the life of the dog. Again, before we can correct undesired behavior, we need to understand where it stems from, at least to the best of our ability. Everything a dog does is based on previous experience, or lack thereof.

Canine Aggression

Canine aggression, just as with most other issues concerning the dog's character, stems from the lack of socialization, specifically the lack of proper imprinting, both within the litter and within the home during the formative time of the dog's life. This is the part of the dog's life when construction and implementation of the parameters concerning social interaction are accomplished.

Though it is highly possible for canine aggression to be exhibited out of fear by the timid dog, and while the dog that is dog aggressive may be one who was allowed to bully others in the litter during the limited time he was there, more often than not, this is a dog that was not socialized at all with other dogs after being removed from the litter. This lack of socialization causes the dog view every other dog is a likely imminent threat.

Unlike the overcompensating dog, this dog is not bluffing. Out of fear, a skewed sense of self-preservation, and possibly even a misplaced sense of social position, the dog will make every attempt to aggressively engage just about any dog he encounters.

It is also not at all uncommon to encounter dogs that are by-products of an environment that encourages this activity. Because some person believed this type of activity expressed strength, courage, or social dominance, dog aggression is often promoted in young dogs, specifically in males of certain breeds.

Regardless whether canine aggression is promoted by the dog's owner, is an act of fear out of timidity, or if it is simply a part of a particular dog's perception of the world around him, we can still trace the roots of the problem to a lack of proper socialization during the dog's early formative window of the dog's life.

The Codependent Dog

While the pack is dependent upon the balance of the members for its very existence, each member has individual duties and responsibilities they are expected to perform. The codependent dog, however, is a dog that would not survive in the wild,

This is yet another condition stemming from poor and improper imprinting early in the dog's life. Typically, when we see a dog exhibiting codependence, we discover that the dog was originally obtained at an early age by the owner and was "cared" for in a manner inconsistent with the dog's needs.

Often, these dogs are ornaments for the owner, or a substitute for a child or spouse.

Early in the dog's life, the dog was coddled and petted, spoken to in "baby talk," and most likely cared for as one would a human infant. This dog was never left alone to establish a sense of self-reliance, learning to cope with being alone for even short amounts of time. Now, it cannot be left alone in a crate, kennel, or even with the run of the entire house without experiencing a great amount of distress.

Often, these dogs will also have a history of being physically carried around by the owner. This carrying of the dog prevents it from learning to develop either physically or mentally to engage obstacles in its path. Whether it is a puppy or a toy breed, carrying the small dog around all the time is doing the dog a huge disservice.

The codependent dog does not possess the confidence or character to engage any task, situation, or scenario on its own. This dog believes that at least the presence, if not the actual assistance of the owner is required to overcome any inconvenience he may encounter.

To counter-condition codependency in dogs, we must create situations and environments that require the dog to make decisions in regard to its own wellbeing, while at the same time fostering a sense of self-reliance.

The Unchecked Dog

The unchecked dog, simply explained, is the dog that has never had any parameters established in regard to acceptable or unacceptable behavior. This type of dog will prove to be more than difficult for the inexperienced handler to deal with as he has been given the opportunity to establish his own guidelines for behavior and interaction. Having received no governing of his behavior, and no establishment of acceptable social parameters, this dog may also appear to be quite aggressive, especially towards other animals.

An unchecked dog that is a couple of years of age or more, will prove quite difficult to work with in even basic obedience. The handler must remember that since the dog has become accustomed to establishing his own operational guidelines, he has had no reason up to this point to follow directions, or to accept any semblance of correction.

As with all of the other conditions we have discussed stemming from poor or lacking imprinting, dealing with this dog will take great amounts of time, patience, and effort on the part of the handler. This dog must have a reason to decide to follow the handler's direction. To attempt to abruptly and forcefully impose these factors on the dog will often lead to either a physical confrontation with the dog, or the dog shutting down.

Most times, especially in the more severe cases in older dogs, the dog will not willingly accept the direction of the handler initially, will begin to first challenge the handler, and will then shut down when it does not have the opportunity to dictate the bounds of operation.

The younger dog will most definitely be much easier to deal with, and with enough time working with the dog, may even prove to be a very nice candidate for the handler.

The OCD Dog

A great number of dogs diagnosed with obsessive compulsive disorders (OCD) have typically been misunderstood and misdiagnosed, and quite frequently prescribed medication such as antidepressants. A portion of these dogs are actually far from suffering from some disorder, but instead exhibiting the traits, drives and characteristics that have been promoted within certain breeds over many generations of selective breeding. Typically, these dogs are representatives of breed categories with elevated levels of certain drives, such as miniatures and toys, terriers, and herding/working breeds.

It is troubling to see the amount of high-drive dogs that are regularly purchased or adopted by people living in apartments, or who lack either the opportunity or desire to spend time with the dog. We see many dogs that are nice representatives of their respective breed, but the owner is unhappy with the dog due to his or her expectation that the animal would basically be nothing more than another piece of furniture in their home. Owners who buy these dogs, then circumvent any opportunity for the dog to truly experience life in a fulfilling and rewarding manner are not only committing an injustice to the dog, but are also creating much larger problems which will become evident in most every facet of the dog and handler relationship.

In most cases, this type of behavior actually stems from excessive energy, and speaks volumes that there is little interaction taking place between the handler and dog on a regular basis. Some of this energy may also be nervous energy, specifically in the toy and miniature breeds. In both cases, these dogs need an outlet for this pent up energy. Simply put; play ball with them, allow them to chase a toy outside, take them on a walk or run with them, but do something with the dog to allow them an outlet for their energy.

Cases do exist, in low numbers, where these types of activities are actually symptoms of an underlying psychological disorder. Historically, these disorders have been by-products of poor breeding. For these conditions that can be diagnosed as valid inconsistencies within the dog's genetic makeup, medication will likely be necessary in order for the dog to live a more comfortable and fair life.

The Environmental Dog

The dog with environmental issues is yet another example of poor, incorrect, or a lack of imprinting. These are the dogs that will appear as solid animals outdoors, but once inside, become fearful and shut down. This may be the dog that will play ball all day long at home, but when taken to another location, will appear scared or fearful, showing little to no interest in the ball. It may be the dog that does well indoors, but only as long as there is carpeting available because he cannot negotiate slick and reflective flooring.

There are numerous examples of the environmental dog, but each are directly attributed to limited or incorrect exposure of the dog to various environments and stimulus early in the dog's life. Dogs with issues when passing through doorways are most likely dogs that were dragged or otherwise forced through doorways during their youth. Dogs that have issues with slick floors typically have not been given ample opportunity to learn how to correctly negotiate these floors. Some dogs that have issues with slick floors may have an undiagnosed vision disease or illness. Dogs that have great issues with exhibiting the same behavior and activity at locations away from home that they readily exhibit in their home environment, have typically had little exposure to the world outside of their own property.

If the dog is still young enough, he can usually be conditioned through most of these problems through positive motivation. Whatever the issues the dog may have with a certain environment, more exposures to this environment must be created for him. These exposures should be short in length at first, and should always be positive for the dog. Playing retrieving games with the dog in and around troubling environments will create a positive association with the environment. With ample time and positive exposures, the young dog with environmental issues can usually recover to the point of being able to operate within these environments.

Just as with other early imprinting conditions, for the dog five years of age or older, the rate of correction for environmental issues can be low. The handler should still work to positively correct these environmental issues. By working positively with the dog in these environments, even if the issue is never completely corrected, over time, the dog should become more comfortable when exposed to these environmental influences.

Gender Aversion

While there are certain dogs that bond more easily with a person of the female gender, and dogs that bond more easily with the male gender, dogs exhibiting gender aversion will take extreme measures to avoid people of one gender over the other.

This can be due to a few different reasons, and this condition, just like the others we have discussed, is rooted in the dog's early history. One selection of these dogs covers those that have been raised or spent most of their lives with a people of one gender. These dogs can typically be worked through their gender aversion issues by use of positive motivation, and creating positive interaction scenarios.

The second selection covers those dogs that have been heavily abused by a particular gender. These dogs will often communicate their disdain for this particular gender of person by exhibiting changes in behavior inconsistent with their normal disposition. This change in behavior may be uncharacteristically aggressive, such as pinning of the ears, baring of the teeth, or even charging at and attempting to physically engage the person. The behavior change may also be uncharacteristically passive, such as the tail between the legs, lowering of the head, cowering, or even becoming as evasive as possible given the situation and environment.

The dogs in this second category may never completely accept people of the gender toward which they have such an aversion, though some progress may be seen in younger dogs through many months and possibly years of positive counter conditioning.

Medical Issues

Thus far, we have discussed various conditions often encountered in the shelter dog. Most of these are traceable to early removal of the dog from the litter and the poor or lacking imprinting in the early life of the dog. We would be remiss, however, if we did not address medical issues when evaluating the various dogs that shelters or rescues may encounter.

We are not discussing the actual medical issues here (which would be a book in and of itself), but to the effects of such afflictions on the dog. It is not uncommon for the shelter or rescue organization to receive a dog into its facility, and then improperly and unnecessarily quarantine it or even euthanize it because of the initial behavior exhibited by it.

My goal in this section is to raise awareness of the importance of properly evaluating dogs completely and competently during intake. I will give just one of the many examples in which a dog faced certain death as a direct result of incompetent evaluation.

I was contacted by a local rescue organization to evaluate a Rottweiler for them. The story I was originally told was that this particular dog had been taken to the veterinarian, that they were told that the dog was three years old, and that he was vicious. “A menace to society” is the exact phrase used to describe this dog. They were told he needed to be euthanized.

The rescue wanted to be certain that the dog was vicious, and knew they needed a second opinion.

As I approached the dog in his crate, I easily noticed that this Rottweiler was nowhere near three years old. We got him out of the crate, and turned him out on a long line to let him stretch and relieve himself. This dog had remarkable character, and was very social. As we began to work with the dog, he allowed us to check his teeth. He was only ten months old.

As he walked around, his hindquarters caught my attention. As I began to check him out more, it became apparent that he had a dislocated hip. This dog would leap and jump up, wanting interaction with each of us that was present. Even with this dislocation, the dog sought our attention. It was very apparent that the dog enjoyed the interaction. Just the day before, he had been labeled a vicious menace, and given a date for death!

This dog came to stay with us until the day before his surgery. As it turns out, he had undergone a prior surgery on this same hip, and had the pins and screws in his leg to prove it (according to the preliminary x-rays taken before his surgery). He underwent the hip surgery, recovered well, and was placed in a home where he could live a fulfilling life.

This dog was clearly misunderstood, and was not vicious at all. In all actuality, this dog had a wonderful personality, interacted well with other dogs, and was trustworthy with children.

Again, as professionals in this field, we undertake the responsibility for providing adequate care and concern for each of the animals under our charge. Because this dog was a Rottweiler, there existed a prejudice that he was a bad dog. As a result, no competent evaluation was given, to the extent that a ten month old puppy was labeled a three year old adult.

We can also surmise that the handling of this dog during the veterinarian's evaluation, specifically because of this pre-disposition, was most probably quite rough. If this dog, while suffering from a dislocated hip, was handled roughly or manipulated in such manner as to create greater pain for him, it is easy to understand the negative activity he would most likely (and justifiably) have exhibited.

Medical conditions can cause many adverse reactions, in regards to attitude and disposition, in dogs just as they do for humans. When evaluating dogs during the intake process, make very sure that the evaluation is not given under a predisposition because of breed. Just as important, make sure the dog does not receive a designation based upon a symptom of a greater underlying problem.

Chapter Twelve

Adopting a Dog to a Working Environment

I have often worked with rescues throughout the U.S., helping them place dogs that exhibit the certain traits, drives, and characteristics necessary in a working dog. By working dog, I am referring to dogs conditioned to work in advanced fields of service including, but not limited to: Search and Rescue, Narcotics, Contraband, Explosives, Mold, Arson, and Assistance Dogs.

Adopting a dog to a working environment can be somewhat controversial. Having worked in the Shelter/Rescue/Investigation forum, I can recall many varied and interesting situations, but most important was the opportunity to interact with so many wonderful dogs.

Once such dog, I will call him Dillon, was a wonderful Yellow Labrador who had been adopted out more than once, only to be returned to the shelter shortly after each adoption. Dillon had an extreme level of both prey and social drive. While these had been the root of his issues in the adoptive homes, they were the very attributes that would allow him to perform the duties of a working dog successfully. If Dillon had one trying characteristic, it was the fact that he was also an accomplished fence climber, expressing his desire to do whatever was necessary to be with those whom he loved.

This particular shelter was contacted by a police officer looking for a dog to enter into a narcotics detection course, and ultimately serve as his K9 partner. He came to visit and work with Dillon several times before committing to him, which I have to admit, impressed me a little. Still, I had concerns and shared them with him. Utmost was that at that particular time, it was common for law enforcement dogs to go to work, and then be sequestered to the backyard at the end of the day. This dog would not be satisfied with being alone in the backyard.

Dillon's adoption was approved through the typical adoption chain, and I never saw him again. It was later discovered that Dillon had been chained out in the backyard and, due to the fact that he was a fence climber, he escaped. He was later found dead on the side of the road, after being hit by a car. Dillon was a top-notch dog, one of the few good Labs left in our country. He had the capability to not only locate narcotics in schools and on our streets, but to do so with great proficiency. He could've made a difference, but was robbed of that chance by someone who lacked the prerequisites every handler and pet owner should have.

When contacted by either individuals or facilities interested in adopting a dog for placement into a working environment, I feel it is important to request a visit to their training facility. If the opportunity exists, I ask to see their personal dog work, as well as attend some of their training events. I understand this can be very time-consuming, however, I also know there are many trainers out there that recommend the "helicopter" method of training. In this method, the choke chain or prong collar is placed around the dog's neck, hooked to the leash, and the dog is then lifted off the ground by the leash and spun around, rotating around the handler until the dog gives out. Once the dog sits, he or she is then told, "Good Dog." Some facilities teach that to get the dog to down, you loop the lead under your foot and then pull upwards with the handle end of the leash, snatching the dog into a down position, and again, then he or she is again told, "Good Dog."

Some facilities also now teach that you must have an electric collar on the dog in order to teach the recall. The recall is a simple exercise where you call the dog to you and he/she comes running. These people actually call the dog to them and shock the dog via the electric collar the entire time he is running to the handler. Once the dog arrives at the handler and gets into proper position, the shock stops. If one has to shock the dog to get the dog to come to them in the first place, what is the missing primary component? COMMUNICATION!

The dog's primary desire is to please us. He is born into this work to function as a pack member, one whose mere survival depends on functioning as a contributing member of the Team. Through the dog's simplistic view, this is what he understands, as this is the way God created the species. Where in the example above is the idea of Team or Partner?

We get calls and emails frequently from shelters, rescues and private individuals to see if we have any "jobs" available for dogs. While this is pleasing, it can sometimes also be quite frustrating. It can be difficult at times to locate the appropriate handlers or to construct a working relationship with those who exhibit the Three Prerequisites we teach. We cannot, in good conscience, put a dog into a situation where he is set up to fail. We have, however, been extremely blessed in many situations where we have been able to assist in the proper placement of many shelter and rescue dogs. They now live their lives performing a service, and are also included as an integral part of their new families.

When dogs come to us through any of the various rescues we normally deal with, typically, the people involved with these organizations are familiar with how we operate and understand the ground that we stand on. If not, we encourage them to make arrangements to come out to meet us. If for some reason the dog fails, the dog either can go back to the rescue for placement, or stay with us while we assist in its placement. While I prefer that the dog stay with us until the right home is found, in the real world that cannot always be the case. Regardless, it is by working together as a Team that proper placement can be found.

It is commonplace for shelter and rescue organizations to be a bit leery of adopting dogs out to working environments—just as they should be. However, if done correctly, I hope you can understand this can be highly successful for and rewarding to the dog, as well as advantageous to the organization itself.

Chapter Thirteen

Search and Rescue/ Recovery (SAR): The Dual Deployment K9

There has always been considerable debate as to the deployment of SAR dogs which have been conditioned to locate both live and deceased victims. Each discipline serves an important, necessary and vital role under the umbrella of SAR, and each has specific function as well as deployment protocol.

To begin, when deploying the dog which has been conditioned to locate both live and deceased human beings, there is a conflict of direction within the dog. Attempting to separate the dog from this conflict by the use of separate commands for each aspect, though often seen as "the" answer, becomes moot once the search process begins. The dog is deployed in the same relevant environment, and basically, the same protocol is followed. When the dog begins to search, after being conditioned to locate either odor base, he will continue to search for either odor base, and will respond to the first one he approaches.

Contrary to this popular approach, you simply cannot correct the dog for locating and alerting to the presence of one odor just because the search has been initiated for the other. Doing so will prove detrimental in training/working the dog when you wish for him to reliably locate and alert on such odor. For you have, in fact, already corrected him, in essence telling the dog "this odor is no longer what we will search for." Hence, a major conflict in working has been instilled by the handler.

We also cannot reliably and responsibly depend upon a different alert activity from the dog based upon the particular find. Understanding there are no perfect handlers, and there are no perfect dogs, it is only rational to understand that either can make mistakes.

If the handler misinterprets the dog's alert, or the dog exhibits an alert contrary to the normal alert for the odor which he has found, this may be a result of stress, anxiety, frustration, or fatigue. At this point, the alert will be taken by the handler and SAR Incident Commander (or representative) as justification to progress to the next tier of rescue in that particular location in an attempt to remove the victim.

Secondly, taking into account the aforementioned contradictions, one must address deployment issues with these particular K9 Teams.

The location of live people and location of deceased people are two completely separate and opposite missions undertaken by SAR Teams. The number one priority of any Search and Rescue team must be the preservation of human life. Only after all possibilities of locating all surviving victims (RESCUE) have been exhausted must the command level decision be made to begin the detection and location of the deceased (RECOVERY).

If these separations in mission responsibility and deployment protocol are not made, countless issues will plague the search effort. In any event which can be classified as a mass casualty event (plane crash, train derailment, tornado, hurricane, building collapse, flooding, bombing, etc.), the assumptions of and prior planning for the protocol of the search must account for the implementation and utilization of two separate missions: Rescue and Recovery.

If the dog which is cross-conditioned for both live and deceased persons is deployed, the percentage of possibilities for the dog to alert on the deceased are just as high as for the possibilities of the dog to alert on trapped, live victims. We do not know at the time of the cross-conditioned dog's alert if this is a still living victim, or one who has perished during the event. The result of this, since only the dog . have alerted on and why, is that valuable resou. devoted to the uncovering and removal of debris in locate that on which the dog has alerted.

There are two primary concerns involved here: The first and foremost is that we have potentially failed in our moral and ethical obligations to victims' families (which we assumed by performing SAR work) by allowing a living victim to expire while searching for a deceased victim upon whom our canine has alerted. The second consideration is one of legal liability for deploying an improperly prepared team under the pretense of saving lives, then actually doing the opposite.

Though we must hold the location and respectful removal of deceased persons as a high priority, this can in no way interfere or even delay the location and rescue of living victims. By failing to do so, we lose the primary focus and intent of Search and Rescue—to save human lives.

The decision to change our mission priority from Rescue to one dedicated to Recovery is made as a directive given by the SAR Incident Command System (ICS). This decision can only be made after careful consideration is given to a compilation of various mitigating factors, including, but not limited to: the type of event, the severity or intensity of the event, the possibility of survivors, and the amount of time that has transpired since the onset of the particular event.

Those individuals currently operating with K9's conditioned to locate both live and deceased victims will ultimately bring peril to those who may have otherwise been located and rescued by the mission-specific team. Essentially, SAR ICS faces two separate missions, which translates into the necessity of deploying two separate, yet equally important types of dog teams, and to deploy each one appropriately.

The common preface of, "but my dog can," is contradictory to the mission, purpose and collective goals of SAR; to preserve human life. The K9 handler, who, despite his proper training, chooses to undertake a conditioning regime which promotes the ideas of training to locate both live and deceased persons, is conducting himself selfishly. Such a handler will deprive SAR ICS with complete definition of their alerts, and most importantly, will create a working environment which proves inefficient and ineffective in the timely location and preservation of human life.

Chapter Fourteen

Animal Cruelty and Neglect

There seems to be such a vague definition of animal cruelty and neglect in our society today. What actions, activities, or environments define neglect, cruelty, or abuse? Where has society gone wrong? What has changed the view of what constitutes animal abuse? How have we come to accept less than acceptable standards for the keeping and working of animals? Where does one begin with making progress to improve the lives of our domesticated companions and partners who depend on us for their everyday survival?

We must first ask ourselves how we, as a society, have ended up here, with such widespread cruel and inhumane treatment of these animals.

I can actually remember a time when more people believed the use of choke chains, pinch collars, and electric shock collars to be unacceptable. You rarely encounter such people anymore. It has now become acceptable to promote choke chains, pinch collars, and shock collars in the conditioning of the dog, forgetting our very fundamental methods that allowed for the domestication of the dog. Attend almost any dog training class and one of these devices will be immediately recommended to you. Strangely enough, companies that manufacture these products even make them for miniature and toy breeds!

There are numerous local, state, and federally funded shelter/rescue/humane society operations across the country that are operating in conditions far from conducive to the positive and fulfilling lives of the animals under their charge, yet a blind eye is turned because of position, association, or affiliation. I have witnessed animals being euthanized that simply did not need it. Conversely, far too many specimens for which euthanasia would be the most humane solution are denied, kept alive to suffer their afflictions.

There are those who, in the course of their official duties, are a bit overzealous in their use of catchpoles. Whether intentionally or not, they leave many animals traumatized as a result of the improper use of this tool. I have witnessed this many times in several facilities just in our state alone. It is quite a disgrace. Some of these individuals clearly have something to prove, while others are simply terrified of dealing with the dog because of either poor (or no) education and training. As a result, the dog is once again not only misunderstood, but ultimately mistreated.

If it is considered unethical, not to mention unhealthy, for a dog to lie in urine and feces in a home or yard, then why is it apparently acceptable in many shelter/rescue environments to allow dogs to do so? (If it doesn't have steam escaping from it, then it has been there too long!) I have observed dogs lying in urine in even highly regarded shelter environments, resulting in dogs suffering staph infections derived from their testicles being constantly exposed to the wet, bacteria infested concrete. When the staff was questioned about this problem, the only response was excuses for why urine was present in the first place. In some cases, the "rescue" dog ends up in more revolting conditions than the previous environment from which it had been "rescued."

There are dogs that spend most of their day inside a kennel; either sharing living space with other dogs with which they are incompatible, or alone with no interaction at all. Yet these very dogs are yelled at or get their kennel gate kicked when they seek interaction by barking and jumping when someone walks by. This actually creates negative cards in the dogs that are in conflict with their societal and play drives—drives that should actually be desired. The dog's behavior merely exhibited eagerness to communicate and interact, as well as a level of confidence. So for a handler to exhibit yelling at the dog or kicking the kennel gate of the shelter/rescue dog is simply unacceptable, even if the dog is barking or jumping in an aggressive manner. In a situation such as this, by yelling and/or kicking the gate or kennel, the handler poses a threat to the dog, most likely driving him further into defense mode.

In all honesty, this handler probably deserves to be bitten. Sometimes the best lessons and corrections come from the dog. And in such instances, it often seems that great respect is earned.

There are also the dogs whose digestive tracts stay messed up due to constant diet change. While I agree any dog food is better than none, in some cases, we must also remain aware of the damage a dog can undergo from constant intestinal stress due to changing food too often. Such intestinal stress can also be caused by providing the dog with food that is comprised primarily of whole corn, corn meal, by-products and fillers.

It also amazes me how such facilities leave water standing in large basins all summer long (and then they wonder why all their dogs have contracted heartworms!). If personnel at such facilities do not know that standing water provides the optimum breeding ground for the mosquito (the spreader of this disease), then they should not be in this business. How can such an environment not be classified as neglectful?

As to heartworms, there are facilities that take in heartworm positive dogs every day, a by-product of owner irresponsibility, never seeking compensation from the owner for treatment of such. Does this not remove the initial owner's responsibility and accountability? What a quandary.

It has also become acceptable for trainers in our country to use the "helicopter" method of dog training. Often, handlers will bring dogs to us to undergo and participate in our various training courses. Just as often, many of these very nice dogs that would have had almost unlimited potential, reach us only after being ruined by individuals in our country who use the "helicopter" and other methods to condition canines. The handlers are often as confused as the dogs!

It seems to be acceptable for dogs to be tethered outside to a tree for the majority of their lives, as long as they have shelter, food, and water. This is not only wrong, but it is neglectful as well. Such a dog is being denied the interaction and stimulation essential to its development and socialization. By being "tied out," the dog is not only subjected to the various climate conditions, but suffer from increased levels of disease and notoriously high levels of both internal and external parasites. In addition, the tied-out dog is sitting prey-in-wait for other dogs, and thus tormented by every passing person, animal and automobile.

I am not stating that keeping a dog outside is necessarily wrong. However, the dog should be kept in a contained area that is of suitable size and construction for it. If the dog is a fence climber, invest in a crate and keep the dog inside.

Typically, fence climbers are dogs that simply need exercise, interaction, and direction. They seek communication, acceptance, approval, and need an outlet to burn off stress, such as chasing a ball. Yet, what has happened is people have once again lost respect for the dog, and have taken the easiest route possible.

In a recent local radio broadcast they featured "professional" dog trainers (whose names I won't mention), taking phone calls about animal behavior issues and such. One caller with a 10 week old Doberman Pinscher puppy was having issues with his puppy biting at his ankles while walking. I want you to know these trainers actually recommended hitting the puppy in the nose to prevent this behavior from recurring. This is so frustrating to me that this was not only accepted, but revered by the caller as a "great suggestion."

Though these individuals are referred to as professionals in this field of work, not one time did they mention pack structure to the owner of the puppy. Nor did they attempt to cover how to properly correct this behavior on a level the puppy could understand. Not one time did they mention the teething process and how this could be a contributing factor as well. They did not mention the interaction the puppy needs, how to focus such behavior, or how to create an outlet for the boundless puppy energy, including owner interaction. Not one time did they mention any of this. They merely instructed the caller to hit the dog on the nose to correct the behavior and that was it.

This puppy will grow into an adult that will cower when a hand is raised or that will become callous to such rude behavior and eventually take action against it. Once the dog reaches this point, he will be labeled a menace to society and be euthanized because he is unsafe, not trustworthy, or just plain vicious. In turn, these types of actions and the resulting reactions will lead to breed banning of the Doberman Pincher in not only our state, but throughout our country as well. This type of poor education has to be dealt with.

Recently, I viewed an episode of one of the many popular cop shows that air on television. On this particular show, there was a call-out for law enforcement to assist at a residence that had a black snake on the porch. After the non-venomous snake had been sprayed with pepper gas, one of the officers approached it and beat it to death with his baton. After doing so, he walked away and stated "That's how you take care of a snake. That's how you do it—you hit them in the head." This exhibit of machismo was quite pitiful, revealing personal insecurity and a definite lack of respect for the animal. If the law enforcement officer had no training or education under his belt on how to deal with such situations, why is he allowed to take charge of the response, and who is held accountable for such decisions?

Again, exactly what actions fall under "animal cruelty" and "neglect"? Are cruelty and neglect only considered as such when committed by private individuals in our society, and not so when committed under some color of authority? How many children in our country do you think saw this? What does this say to the children that we will one day depend upon to legislate and represent our country?

Every incorporated city large enough to staff a police department should employ an Animal Control Officer. It is completely justifiable. The Animal Control Officer should have proper training and education regarding animal cruelty and neglect, and animal husbandry. Their training should not only include domesticated animals but also wildlife indigenous to their area. It should also include basic anatomy and physiology of species which may be encountered, emergency care, illness, disease, and parasitic conditions. It surely wouldn't hurt for these officers to have a basic understanding of dog breeds, at least the most commonly encountered breeds, because, contrary to belief, not every dog in a shelter or pound is a Shepherd or Lab cross.

It should be the responsibility of the Animal Control Officer to assist with the caring for or rescue of animals in distress and to investigate animal nuisance complaints, to include those concerning vicious dogs, and to assist with the proper disposal of the carcasses of deceased animals. It should also be within the scope of operation for the Animal Control Officer to teach the responsibilities of dog ownership, as well as leash laws and tether laws.

I do not necessarily feel that Animal Cruelty and Neglect Investigators need to be employed by individual humane societies or rescue organizations. The Animal Cruelty and Neglect Investigator needs to be hired by the state, county or possibly even a city (depending upon size and population base), and his or her office should be located within the investigative division of that city or county. The primary reason for this is the removal of conflict of interest issues when an investigation involves neighboring humane societies or rescue organizations, or if an investigation needs to be performed on the humane society or organization the investigator would have been employed by.

I also do not feel the Animal Cruelty and Neglect Investigator should hold any seat on the Board of Directors or participate in any committee of such society or organization, as there needs to be a clear and definite separation of ties and responsibilities to insure proper ethics.

The Animal Cruelty and Neglect Investigator should also have relevant instruction to include: investigative techniques and protocol, courtroom testimony, case law, accumulation of documentation, and be educated in the local, state, and federal legal aspects of animal cruelty and neglect. This individual should also be educated in animal husbandry, inclusive of livestock, wildlife, and exotics, as well as anatomy and physiology, emergency care, illness, disease, and parasitic conditions.

This investigator should be educated in recognizing the traits common in both criminal human behavior as well as animal behavior. They should receive instruction in self-defense against both, and receive proper instruction and training in carrying the weapon and its proper use. It should be the responsibility of the Animal Cruelty and Neglect Investigator to work alongside and present sufficient documentation of the Animal Control Officer, if working within his or her jurisdiction, or when pursuing the investigative process from inception through prosecution when outside the incorporated areas of the county.

In addition, it should also be the responsibility of the Animal Cruelty and Neglect Investigator to pursue the issue of warrant of seizure, as applicable, for animals of abuse and neglect and/or warrant of arrest for those responsible for and/or knowingly participating in such acts. As difficult as this type of work may be, there is no room for careless mistakes, pity, or emotional conflict during the actual seizure of animals living in or possibly even suffering severely from cruelty and neglect. After all, their well-being is dependent upon professionals in this field conducting their duties in a thoughtful, professional manner.

All seizures of such animals should be executed not only by the Animal Cruelty and Neglect Investigator and Animal

Control Officer (as applicable), but preferably along with at least two additional officers from the law enforcement agency holding jurisdiction over such operations. These additional officers are to assist with the seizure process, provide witness testimony, and possibly even control bystanders in the surrounding environment who try to intervene in the process.

We must remember that while we cannot ever legislate morality or decency, we can educate.

Chapter Fifteen

Spay and Neuter

Myth

Myth: Spaying or neutering your pet will prevent your dog from roaming, or from running away.

Myth: Spaying or neutering your pet will prevent food aggression.

Myth: Spaying or neutering your pet will prevent dog aggression.

Myth: Spaying or neutering your pet will reduce chances of biting.

Myth: Spaying or neutering your pet will prevent territorial marking.

Myth: Spaying or neutering your pet will curb hyperactivity, or will hamper drive.

Myth: Spaying or neutering makes pets better, more affectionate companions.

Fact

Fact: Neutering will remove all possibilities of testicular cancer.

Fact: Spaying will remove all possibilities of ovarian and uterine cancer.

Fact: Neutering the dog before the age of one year (sometimes even older), removes the possibility of proper growth, including a proportionately sized head, neck, shoulders, pelvis, skeleton and muscular formation.

Fact: Spaying the bitch before the age of one year (sometimes even older) prevents proper feminine growth to include strong defined hips, neck, pelvis, skeleton and muscular formation.

The fact is, if dog owners were not irresponsible in the first place, the need to spay and neuter would be very limited. Too many dogs are spayed and neutered for the wrong reasons in our country, and the larger balance of the myths listed above refer primarily to behavioral issues, not reproductive ones.

The term "fixed" has become the most commonly used terminology when referring to spay or neuter, when in reality, the dog is not "broken." Over the last number of years, the pet-owning public has been conditioned to accept not only the application of this terminology, but the accompanying thought processes attached to it.

That process goes something like this: If you own a pet, not only is this animal "broken" for possessing the very reproductive organs God created for them, but they are uncontrollable, undependable, irresponsible breeding machines that will kill or maim every person who stands in their way. Further, the pet owner (you), is wrong and will be a social outcast for allowing the continued existence of this animal in such condition.

We must refuse to use the terminology, "fixed," when referring to the sterilization process, and come to terms with the fact that the dog is not broken. It is surprising how many adults do not even know the correct application for the terms "spay" and "neuter." There is little acknowledgement that these are two separate, completely different surgical procedures and apply specifically to male and female anatomy, as applicable.

Along with the use of "fixed" as a replacement of the correct, applicable terminology, comes a much more attractive light being shed on having the dog undergo this procedure. No longer is there conscious thought that this is a surgical procedure requiring the sedation of the dog, cutting of the dog with a scalpel, cutting and removal of the reproductive organs, sewing of tissue, and the resulting soreness and recovery process.

Using the term, "fixed," affords a bit more detachment from the actual events that are about to take place on the dog's body because it seems not only the right and acceptable thing to do in today's society. We have removed from the discussion the trauma we are forcing on the dog.

This is not like taking your car to get the brakes "fixed," dropping it off in the morning, picking it up in the afternoon, the worn or defective parts replaced, and the car now serviceable and safe. Yet that has become the popular attitude towards spay and neuter. Simply drop the "broken" animal off at the clinic on your way to work, and in the afternoon, you can pick up your "fixed" dog—now presumably safe and trouble- free.

In addition, with all of the preaching about spaying and neutering, it has actually been programmed into society that you no longer have to be responsible for the animal. Think about this for a minute. When you spay the bitch, she cannot get pregnant. When you neuter the dog, he cannot cause pregnancy. If people were responsible and kept the bitch in heat contained and supervised, she could not be bred. If the male dog is supervised, he would not have the opportunity to breed. However, the irresponsibility of dog owners contributes to the excessive, unwanted, and often, unhealthy breeding, resulting in more strays that either end up as road kill, or overpopulate the shelter industry.

I recall a remarkable seven year old client who owned a five year old unaltered female Labrador, named Lizzy. This little girl could, with confidence, educate others as to the reproductive system function and cycle of the female dog, as well as how to be a responsible pet owner by preventing unwanted litters, without taking the easy way out, with spay and neuter. So for those of you who are irresponsible pet owners, filling up our streets and shelters with unwanted litters, you might want to think about this.

By mandating spay and neuter, we take this level of responsibility away from the dog owner. If the reproductive capabilities no longer exist, then the owner of such dog has no concern of responsibility for an unwanted litter, and thus, allows their "safe" dog to run free on their own. And why not? The dog cannot contribute to the population issue, right? This says nothing about chasing the neighbor's cat, tearing into garbage, leaving their poop in someone else's yard, nor does the "fix" make the dog immune to the effects of a four thousand pound automobile.

We are faced with regulations that make spaying and neutering mandatory for all animals before they can be made available for adoption in shelters and rescue organizations. While on its face, this may look good, it really is not. The single, most common answer we receive from shelters and rescues when we question why they participate in such a policy is, "Well, you just would not believe how irresponsible some of the people are when they come to our place." This is not an answer—it is an excuse, and such a widespread, almost textbook level response that we hear the exact same thing from different organizations throughout the country. If the shelter or rescue believes the people adopting a particular dog are that irresponsible, then do tell, why are they allowing such people to adopt them in the first place?

An almost unthinkable amount of money is spent yearly by shelters and rescues for the spaying and neutering of cats and dogs whose previous guardian was irresponsible. However, all of the money that goes toward spaying and neutering is not really going to poor, pitiful animals whose life is dependent upon such a procedure. That is secondary. The money is actually paying for the irresponsibility of the careless owners who won't supervise the pet they took on the responsibility of owning.

We are also faced with legislation mandating spaying and neutering of pets between the ages of four to six months old. The animal industry, including shelter and rescue organizations, breeders, professional trainers, and veterinarians must all take a stand against this. This is a huge disservice to the creatures we have domesticated. How can anyone actually consider mandating a surgical procedure that interferes with the dog's natural process of growth and maturity—the ability to be the animal they were domesticated to be? One cannot even properly evaluate a dog for suitability for breeding or for a working field until he or she is at least one year old.

People are irresponsible. Some are irresponsible due to a lack of education. Others are irresponsible by choice.

Though I believe spaying and neutering have become a crutch within our society, removing responsibility and accountability from pet owners, and that is has been misused and overly used, there are situations where the procedures are applicable.

Two reasonable arguments to spay the working female at the appropriate age, are: to prevent distraction of others working alongside her, and, to avoid messes that will need to be cleaned and sanitized during actual deployment. Dogs that have been diagnosed with demodectic mange or various other medical issues should be spayed, neutered, or even euthanized in some cases, to prevent a life of intense suffering. However, this is a decision the veterinarian and owner must make, not mandated by law.

I am sure we all wish we had the solution to this overwhelming problem in our society. How nice it would be to be able to say "and that's it, all in a nutshell," and just fix the whole thing. I do feel, however, that we all agree that education is a good start.

Chapter Sixteen

Breeding

It has become commonplace for dogs to be bred haphazardly, without the people involved giving much advance thought or consideration to the sizeable investment of time, effort, energy, and money that successful breeding will require. In addition to all of this, the potential breeder must begin, at an early point in the program, to gain the proper education essential not only to succeed, but to produce healthy, thriving dogs as well.

I can recall a time when breeders were more responsible. Preserving a breed's particular drives, traits and characteristics was of the highest priority, profit being secondary. The resulting specimens from their breeding programs were dogs to be proud of, that could readily perform the type of tasking typical of those of their particular breed.

Now, we have backyard breeders who have chosen to participate in this particular venue of the animal industry only so that their children may witness the actual whelping process and experience raising puppies. This is one of the poorest and most irresponsible excuses for intentionally breeding dogs, yet one of the most frequently used. This decision to become a breeder is typically made after investing the least amount of energy possible into learning the particular breed's specific drives, traits, and characteristics that should be present and bred for. Such breeders invest even less time in learning how to achieve these desired drives, traits, and characteristics in the offspring, through complementary breeding.

There are breeders who keep their dogs in kennels for the balance of their lives, never providing the dog with essential nutrition, socialization, and exercise. There are also those who are involved in dog breeding solely for what they believe will be great monetary profit. While in some cases this could be true, these breeders still exhibit little to no concern for the well-being of the breed in general, or for any particular dog. Irresponsible breeders seem to be on every street corner or hanging out in every parking lot trying to get rid of the "problem" they have created.

We received a ten-month-old female German Shepherd the owner brought to use for training. He had purchased the dog from what most would consider a professional breeding facility. Upon her arrival, we began the conditioning process by immediately socializing her with other people and other dogs. This is when I began to notice some issues with this dog.

When we would turn her out to "empty," she would go to the concrete to relieve herself instead of going on the grass. Upon turning her out with other dogs, she would run to find a corner and try to seclude herself.

This dog definitely did not understand normal canine play behavior, nor did she want to participate in any activity with other dogs. After a few of these introductions, she began to come out of her shell and began to interact more.

It became evident that this young dog possessed the potential to be a very nice companion, and quite possibly would excel in advanced work the owner wanted to participate in. This elevated level of activity, fueled by her newfound confidence also allowed me to see her body movement in a much different light.

I noticed her right hip seemed to snap quite often, and she had the ever so noticeable bunny hop, a clear sign of hip dysplasia. After contacting our client, we took the dog to our veterinarian for x-rays.

See the results below.

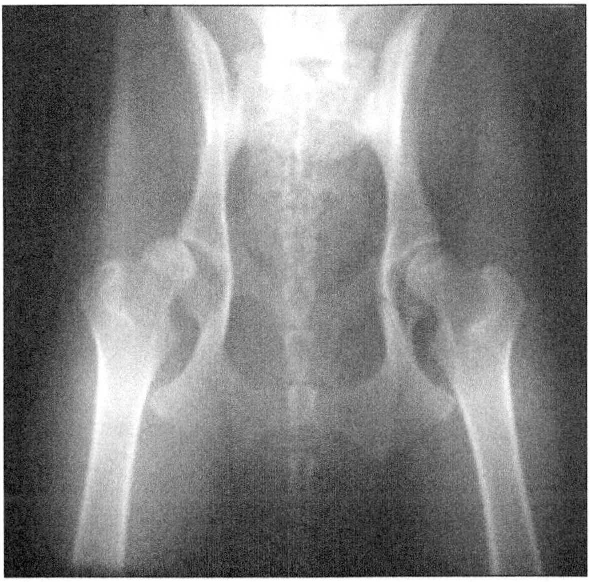

From this picture, the dysplasia in this dog's hips is very evident. Just as striking, this radiograph is of a ten-month-old puppy, and *not* a much older dog that had endured the progression of dysplasia over a number of years.

Take another look.

For comparison, this is an x-ray of a solid hip structure. This particular radiograph was taken of a sixteen-month-old female German Shepherd of approximately the same size.

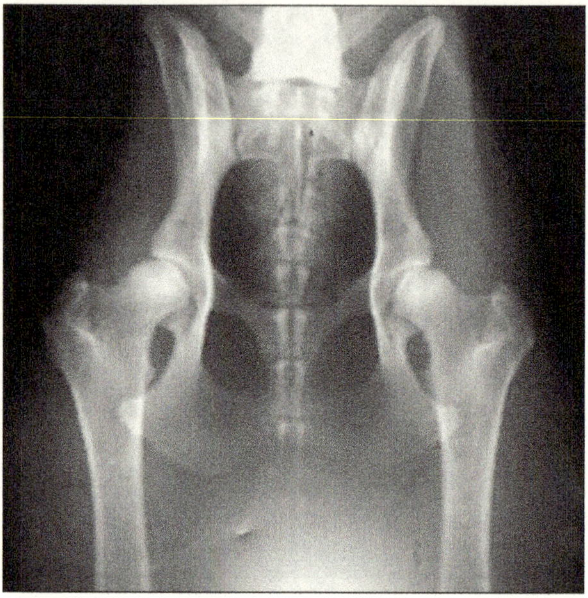

From this x-ray, the well-formed hip joints are evident. Nice, symmetrical formation, with deep, uniform sockets.

From the behavior this particular dog exhibited while with us, it was very apparent to me that the breeders she came from were either in this business for the wrong reasons, or clearly had no idea what they are doing.

For a dog that age to so lack core social skills, it is evident she was separated from the litter at much too early an age. It is also apparent she was placed in a concrete kennel to grow until she was close to the age of one year old. Ironically, this particular kennel, as do many, guarantees hips until the age of one year old as well.

This dog was born with this disease, and with every breath she took, she experienced pain. The level of the severity of her hips proved this. No dog progresses to that stage overnight, yet it seemed the breeders simply turned a blind eye to her, never acknowledging she had an issue. How one, especially the breeder, could not see this is beyond reason, yet this happens all the time.

People, have clearly lost respect for the dog. I fully understand and acknowledge that it is possible to breed two OFA Certified Excellent dogs with the best of intentions and possibly still whelp a puppy that will have hip dysplasia (although even this can be prevented through proper education and research). However, the issue is that this very nice dog was allowed to live life while enduring excruciating pain, and that her condition went unaddressed due to the negligence of irresponsible breeders, as well as that of the trainers who initially began the conditioning process with her.

That very same week, we recommended another client take their nine-month-old Rottweiler in for x-rays, after noticing issues with the dog's mobility. This dog was diagnosed with hip dysplasia as well, but his case was a moderate one, not nearly as severe as the other dog. This dog will endure increasing levels of pain and lowering levels of mobility as he matures and his condition worsens. He will be able to go to a home where he will be cared for, and his level of activity will be kept at mild to moderate. He will never be able to work or perform any of the duties that the Rottweiler was originally bred for. Specifically, he will never be suitable for work as a personal protection dog, and definitely had no future as a potential stud dog, the two primary purposes for which he was originally purchased.

Hip dysplasia has become very common in most working breeds. It has reached the point where one wonders how the dog being bred today could ever begin to meet the same criteria that was once not only required of them, but respected with significant loyalty and gratitude, due to the services the dog provided.

Just as we have breeders who turn a blind eye to the dog every day, there are also registry organizations that have actually promoted the destruction of many breeds in our society today. I have little to no respect for any of these organizations. Some require that you only provide a picture of the dog, then state the breed, gender and date of birth to receive registration papers. They continue to register litters that are most likely carrying bad genes, and are quite obviously opening the door to registering dogs that are not purebred, accurate representations of their respective breeds.

Professional breeders, registry organizations, and backyard breeders alike need to be held both responsible and accountable for their actions (or lack thereof), for they have contributed to the overall demise of the dog, specifically the promulgation of hip and elbow dysplasia. While they continue to speak, write, and promote genetics, animal husbandry, conformation and various other standards, they still make the conscious decision not to address this issue with a realistic approach. Thus this serious issue thrives through an inadequate recognition and registration process that allows bad genes to continue to pass from generation to generation.

We have also accepted the classification of "Pet Quality" dogs. What does it take for people to recognize the true meaning of this? By applying this classification to puppies and young dogs, the breeder is acknowledging that the dog does not exhibit the drives, traits, and characteristics typically associated with the breed. It goes without saying that these dogs cannot pass on what they do not possess, therefore, further diluting the gene pool of the respective breed. These dogs are typically the result of poor breeding programs, yet the breeder will follow through with the sale and placement of these dogs with unsuspecting buyers, in pursuit of making a few more dollars.

There are many rescue and shelter organizations that continuously provide our communities, including our children, with information that is clearly unhealthy. For example, that it is wrong to purchase a dog from a breeder when there are so many poor, helpless animals in shelters. Many people who are interested in purchasing a dog have a particular breed or breeds in mind that they are attracted to. Perhaps they want a dog with a documented medical history, lineage, and genetic profile. It is also possible they do not want to risk owning a diseased dog, one with lifelong medical issues, or one with bad cards and problem-solving behaviors. Regardless of the reason, it is wrong to play upon another's pity and use the "poor, helpless, homeless" dogs in the shelters in an attempt to brainwash children to think that purchasing from a breeder is wrong.

Not all breeders are bad. Many breeders have dedicated their entire lives not only to this industry, but to better the particular breed they are involved with. Many breeders are dedicated animal advocates who stand with the dog against animal cruelty and neglect. They would support shelter and rescue organizations more in this area if they were not constantly being ridiculed by them. The same goes for trainers (but that is not what this chapter is about).

Many breeders, and sometimes retired breeders, also choose to operate breed specific rescue and shelter organizations. By doing so, they provide many years of experience, not only working with that particular breed, but also understanding its specific drives, traits, and characteristics that should be present within specimens of the breed. They are dedicated not only to adopting out those who exhibit an "even" character, but to ensuring the new handler also exhibits "even" character.

The actual art of breeding requires commitment, dedication, proper education, and of course, a fair amount of money. It is an honorable, rewarding profession, when engaged with the dog as the number one priority.

Chapter Seventeen

Bully Breeds and Breed Banning

An undertaking on the order of this book would be incomplete without addressing two of perhaps the most debated issues within the dog community: "bully breeds," and "breed banning."

First, it is important to define "bully breed." Most of these breeds can be traced to, and many contain at least some noticeable traits of the Mastiff, or Mastiff "type" dogs. These dogs were large, powerful animals, bred to be so in order to more effectively and efficiently perform their required duties.

The two breeds most commonly referred to as "Pit" are the American Staffordshire Terrier and the Staffordshire Bull Terrier. These have become associated with the American Bulldog, Presa Canario, Dogo Argentino, and even the Boxer, under the singular categorization, "bully breeds."

Though some of these dogs attribute a portion of their varied history as bait dogs, fighting dogs and/or wild animals in a pit, their very inception and subsequent existence neither stems directly from nor hinges upon these activities.

Originally, many of these types of dogs were bred and kept by butchers specifically to take down and control unruly oxen or other cattle—hence the "bull" or "bully" reference. These large, powerful animals were essential to the day-to-day duties of the butcher, and were considered as valuable a resource and necessary tool of business as the butcher's cleaver.

Some of these butcher's dogs were also used for hunting purposes, benefiting from the dog's already well-defined attributes and skills for capturing and, if necessary, killing their quarry. One must also keep in mind this was before the widespread availability and use of firearms for hunting and that the dog has been used for hunting purposes since the beginning of the domestication process.

A portion of these breeds were originally bred specifically for the hunting of large and often dangerous wild game. The pursuit and subsequent capture of this quarry required a dog of high stamina and endurance, coupled with a very high strength to weight ratio.

The boxer, however, can be traced to inception by the German military as a war dog—a very light, quick, agile and courageous dog, charged with the duties of carrying medical supplies and messages between outposts and through the trenches in both World Wars. Eventually, the Boxer's tasking was increased to include performing as a sentry and guard for the German troops.

With the earlier defined breeds, there exists a definite timeline within their history that involved fighting dogs in a pit (along with other dangerous animals). These fights were commonplace across Europe during the 16th Century, and often held as large gatherings of the upper class. Essentially, these events were as popular as our modern-day boxing events. Prized fighters are shown, exhibited, and each promoted as the better fighter, therefore the safer one on which to place one's bet. Ultimately, the two fighters will face each other in the ring, and the fight will ensue. The difference here is that, routinely, one of these fighters (and quite possibly both), dies in the fight.

Animal fighting (or "pitting"), eventually became viewed as brutal, barbaric, cruel, and inhumane. The blood sport was eventually phased out of view, but not out of existence, sadly. Although various legislative bills and laws have been passed against the proliferation and conduction of the sport, those deeply involved with dog fighting have not given up their beloved sport easily.

Although dog fighting has now been banned in most every civilized country in the world, it still continues today in the back alleys of our cities and the backyards of our neighborhoods.

Though there are no longer officially sanctioned events, there exists an extremely strong network structured around the promotion and performance of these fights, as well as for the promulgation of the animals involved. This network spans the country and reaches into every community. It has evolved into a private society fueled by power, illegal drugs, and money.

The animals used in the current fighting rings barely resemble their ancestors, and are by no means an accurate depiction of what the earlier breeds were actually bred for. Specifically, while the earlier dogs may have been used at times for fighting, they were bred primarily to perform specific tasks that were essential to the society in which they lived.

A majority of these dogs today are severely lacking in social skills as a direct result of irresponsible breeding practices, focused towards promoting antisocial behavior in the dogs. These dogs, from the youngest age, are exposed to cruel, often barbaric mental and physical conditioning.

It is not at all uncommon for these young dogs to be exposed to other dogs fighting. By witnessing this behavior and receiving positive reinforcement for exhibiting any aggressive tendencies towards either of the dogs fighting, the dog rapidly comes to understand that this is not only allowed and acceptable behavior, but, most importantly, the desired behavior to exhibit. Through this process, the young dog is imprinted with the activities in which they are expected to engage.

The young dog may then be beaten or placed with a much older and stronger dog to fight. It may have its neck and muzzle protected by a metal covering, even barbed-wire, to prevent it from receiving deadly injuries (while also preventing it from fighting back).

Though it is widely believed that processes resembling the one above produce a much more courageous and tough fighter, the resulting product is actually a dog which lives in fear. Although it may exhibit what appears to be a self-promoting attitude, confidence, and extreme aggression, these are all symptoms of a great underlying problem. This dog fears everyone, and more specifically, every dog because of the earlier foolhardy conditioning process.

A dog so negatively conditioned comes to believe that every person and every dog is an imminent threat, so in the interest of self-preservation, he must lash out, aggress, engage, and fight as long as necessary. The dog, without obvious provocation, will very often exhibit these actions. It is imperative to understand, however, that the provocation existed early on in the conditioning process of the dog, and has become ingrained in the dog's perception of the world around him. This perception has created a dog that believes there are no other options available for dealing with this particular situation than exhibiting the traits and characteristics instilled and promoted in him through previous experience.

This dog is prevented from ever experiencing a fulfilling life since he can never achieve a true level of comfort in any environment because of his overwhelming fear and concern of imminent threat. This dog is a by-product of people driven by the illusion of control, the acceptance and promotion of violence, and the ever-growing pursuit of power. To these people, fighting dogs are merely disposable pawns in a game of social insolence.

With all this in mind, it is important to remember that there are many dogs within our society that do not fit the mold above. Just because there are people who make the conscious choice to engage in the types of activities outlined above, that does not automatically mean every representative of every breed, or their owners, are evil. Not only is such a broad generalization short sighted, it is narrow-minded and wrong.

While there are unquestionably, a very large number of these dogs who will never be able to function within society, much less within the bounds of a family, we must arrive at a reasonable, responsible solution to the problem (one other than simply wiping out entire breeds). There are many representatives of the various so-called bully breeds that perform many different tasks, from hunter to personal assistant. These conduct their duties while also operating as an integral member of the family involved.

In recent years there has been an ever-growing wave of knee-jerk reactions and rash, thoughtless, shallow decisions in regard to "problem" dogs. As of late, municipalities across the country have enacted bans on the possession of bully breeds and many more are considering similar bans. Some are even working towards enacting legislation requiring such dogs to be spayed or neutered before they reach four months of age.

While we discussed the pros and cons of spay and neuter in a previous chapter, this particular situation opens additional concerns. The bully breeds are being singled out, and if effective, this type of mandatory altering will work, along with breed banning, to completely extinguish not only particular breeds, but also an entire type of dog. There are absolutely zero questions as to the agenda of the people involved with generating, promoting and passing these types of legislation, regardless of how caring and colorful their initial proposal may seem.

The concerns of breed banning are far-reaching. In regard to the bully breeds, this ban is not limited to an actual breed, but extends to a type of dog. How many of these bans also call for the banning of the Boston Terrier, the Pug, or the French Bulldog, who all also fit the loosely defined criteria of the ban? None. Absolutely zero. Primarily because, again, these bans are concerned with a type of dog rather than the breed, and these particular breeds just don't create enough public emotion. This is one of the glaring faults of the banning approach.

Most importantly, we must understand that passing the legislation to ban these dogs is the most difficult part of the process. This process revolves around how much public emotion can be created to support the particular ban. This emotion is created out of fear and lack of education. As long as the general public can be frightened enough through the presentation of "facts," polls, statistics and surveys, the purveyors of such legislation pave the way for its passage. (Never mind that their research, "facts," and statistics are skewed in favor of their agenda, coupled with the inundation of sensationalism via television and newspapers.)

Beyond this point is where the danger lies. Once the ban is in place, specifically bans based upon type, association, or other loosely defined criteria, the amending of this legislation is much easier. That means, once the ban legislation is in place, when another breed type of dog loses public favor, or even the favor of a particular Representative or Senator, the stage has already been set to easily add the breed to the ban.

Breed banning is not the answer for any of the dog issues pressing in today's society. Breed banning amounts to nothing more than selective extermination of a particular type of dog, supported by public emotion that is long on fear and short on education.

The first step towards arriving at a realistic lasting answer, is education. As professionals in this industry, it is our collective obligation to ensure this education is available to the public. It is also incumbent upon us to pursue avenues within our individual scope to stifle the purveyors of myths, fear, and misinformation in regard to dogs.

The second step to this answer is responsibility. At this point in this book, hopefully the canine services professional has at least some insight into the responsibilities we have to the dog, and to this industry as a whole. Part of this responsibility is the constant pursuit of step one: sharing of education. The greater portion of this step is the practicing of responsibility. We must individually put into action the very things we are asking the rest of society to practice.

Canine services professionals have a great opportunity before us to be an example of responsibility for the entire community of dog owners, as to the care, housing, rearing, and conditioning process of the dog. Individuals must make the commitment of responsibility to the dog, as well as to educating their neighbor.

Chapter Eighteen

Journey with Wolves

Through my years of being involved in the animal industry, I have been extremely fortunate to have been involved with many wolves, whether that involvement was due to animal cruelty and neglect, or even the invitation to enter a wolf habitat to study the behavior exhibited within the pack. Some of these experiences were positive and some were negative, but each provided me with a learning experience that has contributed to who I am, and solidified the values I stand for today.

In my younger, much less experienced years, I purchased a wolf cub from a breeder. In my young mind, I thought that if I purchased the wolf cub, I would prevent it from ending up somewhere it did not need to be. In all honesty, I would have purchased them all if I would have had the money, as the breeder had tethered the wolves on chains, attached to trees. The pups were allowed to run free because they would not leave their mother. Allowing the cubs to remain with the mother was somewhat uncommon, as most wolf breeders actually believe that by taking the cub away at the age of three weeks old or younger removed wolf instinct, thus preventing them from becoming too wild. (By the way, that is inaccurate information.)

Though I had intended for the person who would take and care for this wolf, to provide a suitable habitat and raise the cub as appropriately as possible, that is not what happened. The wolf was left tethered on a chain for most of his life, seeking acceptance and interaction that was so important to him. He was shot after breaking his chain to chase animals that had been teasing him, that he considered prey. But he was set up to fail from the beginning. It was a bad decision on my part, one that I determined to never make again. However, the odds were stacked against him the moment he drew his first breath of air. Little did I know back in that day, how that event would ultimately work to lead, guide, and direct me through a life that would include a journey with wolves.

Years ago, I was contacted to assist with the removal and relocation of three wolves, and was subsequently asked to take responsibility for their care and keeping. The necessity of relocating these wolves was a by-product of a divorce, and each of the wolves has been neglected by the spouse who was left to oversee their care.

They wolves were contained in a fenced area that was not quite large enough for them, and the ground covering was nothing but dirt. There were huge dens throughout their fenced area that were very impressive, as they had been meticulously constructed. There were several of them, some with tunnels leading to other dens or to ways of escape. Some of the dens were larger than others, allowing more than one wolf to occupy them at any given time. Some were efficient enough for only one.

Yukon was huge. Standing by my side, his back was at my hip. He was enormous and extremely friendly. He had been very well socialized, and oh, how he was a romancer and a pleaser. He was a gentle giant if ever there was one. He was Alpha of this particular pack, an alpha that had been neutered.

Cheyenne was young, frail, and delicate. She had originally been the property of a truck driver who had purchased her in the northern U.S. I was informed that she had been abused as a cub, and nobody had been able to touch her for years. She was only about two and half years old at the time. She had to be tranquilized for transport.

Loafer was very beautiful, and close to Cheyenne's age. He was friendly, but scared. He did not clearly understand the event taking place, nor did he have any reason to. I requested that he be tranquilized before transport; however, the decision was not mine alone, and was rejected. For Loafer, this habitat was all he had known, and it is crucial to remember this was not a dog, but a wolf.

When we arrived at their new habitat, Yukon was eager to check it out, and did, claiming it all as his own. Cheyenne was still under the effects of the tranquilizer for the most part, which was good for her. We moved her while she was still in her crate, and just unlatched the door for her. Loafer was beyond being stressed. He was salivating excessively and his disposition had totally changed. He found himself a spot to lie down and stayed there. He denied any attempts of interaction at all, and died within the first day.

Yukon and Cheyenne settled in fine. Cheyenne eventually developed enough trust of me that she would come close enough that I could have reached out quickly enough to feel her hair if I had tried, however, that would have been wrong on my part, and would have resulted in destroying any trust she had in me, while pushing her further away. It was not long before dens were constructed with perfection, definitely an impressive sight.

Seasons came and went, and the intriguing experiences as well. Cheyenne was never spayed, but had chosen Yukon as her mate long before I took possession of the two, despite the fact he had been neutered and Loafer had not. Since the wolf only cycles once per year, unlike the dog, which cycles twice a year, Cheyenne had experienced two heat seasons, but would not allow any wolf other than Yukon to breed as this was her mate, chosen for life, even though neither had any conception of the surgical alteration that had taken place previously.

Cheyenne always initiated digging the dens, and typically did this in the spring. Yukon helped from time to time, but she did most of the work. I think he caused more trouble by getting in the way to be honest with you. There were ledges in the den to keep the wolves dry in bad weather. The betas also use them while the cubs are young, to have a getaway, so to speak, while being able to watch over them. This is primal to the wolf during cub rearing.

Yukon would literally play football with the kids in the neighborhood. His disposition was awesome. He was a thinker, and made decisions. One day, he chose to escape the habitat by jumping the fence. He went to the garage, chose an item, picked it up and carried it back to the habitat, jumped back over the fence, and delivered the item to Cheyenne as a gift. He repeated this over and over—he worked hard at it too. We never interrupted his process, as it was very intriguing. Cheyenne accepted each gift with such gratitude. She and Yukon would show extreme amounts of affection to one another during this process, and none of the items were ever destroyed by either of them.

They would also catch prey that traveled through their habitat, such as birds, rabbits, and squirrels. Of course, this was not their only source of food, plenty was provided for them, however, one must understand this is primal to the wolf. Their mere survival depends upon these skills and abilities.

The captured prey was not always eaten after being killed. Quite frequently it was buried, and on occasion, brought as a gift to me upon entering their habitat. At times, the gift would be dropped at my feet, and other times the gift was used for games of tug, or otherwise played with. I am certain that plenty of food was buried throughout their habitat in case they ever needed it.

Since I was not able to touch Cheyenne, she took care of grooming herself. As the weather became warmer, she would shed her coat, speeding up the process by plucking clumps of hair, then carefully placing it in chosen dens for bedding. Yukon and Cheyenne spent a lot of time grooming each other.

Cheyenne spent her life wanting to breed; doing what is natural for the wolf, what is primal and necessary for their very survival. She had chosen a mate who, unbeknownst and not understood by her, was neutered, yet she remained committed to him. One has to wonder the thought process that was in her mind. Did she wonder why she was rejected each year? Did she yearn for the litter of cubs she never had? What went through Yukon's mind, not being able to perform the tasks at hand?

Think about it. Breeding is a natural process, primal, an done upon which they are dependent for mere survival. Yet, in spite of not being able to breed, they both remained so committed to one another, continuously doing things for one another, respecting one another, and going through the dance of impressing the chosen mate. In a humanistic aspect, they never stopped courting one another.

Yukon eventually drew his last breath. He had lived a good, healthy life. Cheyenne went and lay by his side, and died shortly thereafter. She was young and in good health. She died from a broken heart; she died because of the level of dedication she had for Yukon.

Typically, breeders who offer wolf hybrids for sale also support the belief that owning a wolf hybrid is different than owning a dog. It is often stated that an owner of these hybrids need to completely understand pack structure when owning a hybrid. It is my personal opinion that anyone who owns a dog, wolf hybrid or not, needs to have a complete understanding of pack structure. This lack of education and understanding is partly responsible for the many unwanted dogs in our country—dogs that are simply misunderstood.

Breeding wolves, while not having a clue to the genetics, chromosomes, anatomical and physiological being of the wolf itself, let alone the dog, is simply wrong. People have lost respect for the wolf, just as they have for the dog, and quite frankly, for most of the creatures on this earth.

However, wolves are different from the domesticated dog. There are some key differences. For example, the pure wolf will never have a pink nose. There are many reasons for this, one being the light pigmentation would not provide the necessary camouflage for successful hunting, nor would it endure the expose to weather due to being more sensitive to the sun. Dogs that carry this genetic makeup are also more prone to various cancers and other diseases. Knowing this, one can also view various breeds of dogs in a different light.

Female wolves come in season once per year, and never before the age of two years old. This is part of their genetic makeup. The female wolf that is well adjusted and mentally adept, does not even consider leaving the pack until this time. Dogs come in season twice per year, and there are many dogs that may cycle more than that. (There is only one breed of dog that I am aware of that share the cycle once per year: the Basenji). It is in my opinion those dogs are simply a product of poor breeding, and through my experience, I have learned that these particular dogs often have other anatomical or physiological defects as well.

The pure wolf does not have rear dewclaws. Dogs do; however, there are some dogs that are born without them. When present, these are typically removed during the first few days of a dog's life. We now have dogs being born with dewclaw defects, such as double or triple dewclaws. Even though these may be removed, what it does not remove is the genetic fault that caused it in the first place. A genetic fault will rear its ugly head eventually and most likely in more ways than one.

The pad of the pure wolf's feet are not round like the dogs, nor are they close together like the dog's pad. The pads are always black, just as the nails are. Pale, pink pads are a genetic defect as well as lightly pigmented nails. These create problems, and dogs with them are more prone to allergies as well. All pure wolves also have hair between their toes.

Breeders often begin removing puppies from the litter and placing them for sale or adoption between six and eight weeks of age. This is not what is primal to the dog. As has been discussed, the most formal part of learning for the dog, the most important part of his life, is between six and fourteen weeks of age. The window of time when the wolf cub ventures out of the den is between six and eight weeks old, however, the cub is not leaving the pack. The cub is constantly supervised and provided with leadership, guidance, grace, compassion and understanding. As the cub matures, he is constantly exposed to many different situations and environments, including learning to hunt and carry out a successful kill, thus providing a meal necessary for his survival. In most cases, puppies that are sold at six to eight weeks of age simply have the cards stacked against them due to a lack of education and understanding of the species by the new owner and the breeder.

Take a look at the digestive tract of the wolf, and what it ingests for survival. The wolf does not forage in a corn or bean field for its meal. If this were the case, prey drive would be of little to no use to the wolf, becoming almost, if not completely, non-existent. The animals God created do not have primal instincts that are not conducive to their survival. Not one. Society has accepted taking dogs and turning them into vegetarians like themselves. Of course, can do what they want. If you want to be a vegetarian, be one. My best friend is one. But it is wrong to take an animal that is primarily carnivorous, and feed him a vegetable and cardboard diet.

Wolves hunt prey, not gardens. Through the domestication process of the dog, the conflict created with certain primal traits of the dog has not and will never be removed. The majority of the corn, berries, nuts and other forage in the wolf's diet are consumed when the digestive track of the captured prey is consumed, and actually comprise a very small percentage of their diet.

The companies that provide cheap dog food, (just as the consumers who purchase it), have either lost respect for the dog or, simply lack a complete understanding of the animal. Ask almost any senior veterinarian how much degenerative disease and illnesses they used to see before the widespread consumption of commercial dog food. There has been a definite increase in diseases in dogs since then: irritable bowel syndrome, cancer, tumors, which all ultimately break down the dog's immune system, resulting in more illness. Yet, society seems to be OK with this.

If one can begin to truly understand the wolf, learn from the wolf, and grow from what is learned, one can gain a new perspective on life. The way they deal with their young is exactly how we should deal with ours, by exhibiting leadership, guidance, grace, compassion, and understanding, while being firm, fair and consistent. Understanding and applying this type of communication creates a greater propensity for successful relationships with one's spouse, child, dog, or even God.

Chapter Nineteen

Animal Education

Animal education needs to stem from honest, true, and forthright communication, and be directed to many different levels of society. I was very fortunate to have been taught from a very early age about many different species of animals, their habitats, and their survival skills. I was taught to respect the animals that have been given to us, and that each has a purpose that serves within our ecosystem.

I was conditioned over the course of most of my life to understand certain animal species, including the dog, which has not only taught me respect for the animal, but also has provided me the information and education necessary to understand them from their perspective. My cards were created early on, and have been continuously stamped through experience and exposure in positive and even sometimes in negative ways. Do not misunderstand when I say "negative experiences." Certain negative experiences offer wonderful learning experiences that ultimately bring about positive influences for later exposures.

Society has not had many opportunities to grab hold of my Rolodex and program me in a way that is contradictory to the way our God created the animals. As you well know, this is not the case for many children in our society today. This saddens me for many different reasons, one being the fact that our country, our world, and our future, which includes the animals that God gave us dominion over, will eventually be held in their hands.

Working with children of all ages is not only extremely rewarding, but also necessary in order to make a difference in not only the individual lives of our youth, but within society as a whole. We actually have clients, children, who train with us in various disciplines we offer, such as obedience, confidence building, search and rescue, and in some cases, even personal protection. These young handlers are some of our best clients, and perform with their partners flawlessly, often exceeding those who have been in this industry for years. The obvious explanation behind this is that these young handlers neither have preconceived notions of conditioning the dog by use of force and compulsion, nor of the relationship required with the dog in order to excel in their training.

Children should be educated properly and according to their maturity level. Children's education should include programs structured around teaching proper responsibilities in all facets of pet ownership (instead of brainwashing them with "spay and neuter"). There is nothing wrong with children of most any age being taught the reproductive process from conception to whelping, as long as it is presented to them at their level of understanding. I do not feel that we should teach children that the actual act of breeding is a bad thing, or that breeding is wrong.

The bottom line is that if people had more respect for the animal, and were more responsible, we wouldn't need to dedicate as much money to support spay and neuter. The money saved could be put toward other campaigns and means necessary to enforce laws in order to hold people accountable for their acts of animal cruelty and neglect. There would also be more funds available for proper education and animal medical care, as well as toward payroll for employees who exhibit the prerequisites that should be required of the animal caretaker/handler.

Children should be taught the domestication process of the Canis lupus familiaris, animal safety, and not only ways that animals help people, but also ways that people help animals. There should also be breed-specific programs that provide education on that particular breed's ancestry and origin: what the breed was originally bred for, as well as if the particular breed may be experiencing societal influences which are adversely altering its established traits, drives, and characteristics.

Children are now being taught that it is OK to hit a puppy on the nose, and that it is acceptable for a pack member, and integral part of the family (the dog), to roam at will, exhibiting little to no dedication or commitment to the family. Children are being taught that force and compulsion is an acceptable way of communicating to an animal—an animal that should be their best friend. Children are also being taught to take the easy way to prevent unwanted conception, instead of being taught how to be responsible animal owners and being held accountable for poor or irresponsible breeding practices. Children are being taught disrespect.

I have received so many phone calls because a dog nipped at a child, and in some cases, the child was actually bitten, not viciously, but the skin may have been broken. The child had pulled the dog's ear, stepped on its tail, gotten into its food dish, or basically been allowed to torment the animal until it decided enough was enough. For the child, it was a negative experience that, in most cases, transformed into a learning experience that created positive, more respectful activity from the child in future exposures.

Most children who receive such correction from a pet typically gain a higher level of understanding of the space and privacy of others—"put in their place" as you might say. The child gains respect and never displays the undesired or disrespectful behavior again. Of course, in many situations, the dog is the one that is immediately labeled "bad," and quickly punished.

Proper education also needs to be provided to the animal industry as a whole. The industry has fallen prey to fast money, so "shortcuts" like force and compulsion techniques have become acceptable without regard to the detriment of the animal. Such shortcuts have ended up "short-cutting" proper owner training, leading them to believe that those techniques are the way is "has to be done." Because the lure of easy money is so great, I have concluded that the way to defeat these practices is by educating you, the consumer and dog owner, that they are not the way it has to be done. If we stand with the dog, those practices will become as unacceptable as they once were and our lives will be even more enriched by developing proper, meaningful and rewarding relationships with our canines.

When a trainer tries to sell you a prong collar, simply walk away, knowing your dog neither deserves nor requires pain to do what you want. In fact, your dog wants to do what you want more than that trainer will ever understand. You simply need to communicate on its level and the results will abound.

Proper education needs to be provided to many veterinarians and veterinarian technicians. Most veterinarians actually welcome education dealing with behavior modification of the dog, and typically understand certain things in a different light once the information is provided.

Those who are presenting bills to the legislature involving bully breeds and breed banning need to be educated properly. People presenting legislation should represent the best interests of the animals concerned. They should not be people with little or no dog education behind them to validate or discard the claims or recommendations made by those who risk destroying breeds. They should not be people who add this issue to their political agenda simply as a hobby or part-timer.

Either way, a legislator with no animal training or education simply has no business dictating to anyone the appropriate measures to take in regard to dealing with a dog or any other animal. Those who are interested in these issues seriously need to spend time in the field dealing first-hand with the animals they seek to ban with their legislation, or receive their advice from a professional who is committed to the wellbeing and promotion of the animals in question.

At the end of the day, the one taking on this serious obligation needs to first meet the prerequisites required of any animal owner or handler in order to be effective in the undertaking. They must seek betterment and protection for the animals entailed within the bounds of their legislation.

DEDICATION

A Short Story of the Inspiring and Wonderful Life of

My Great Grandfather
Ben Hale

My Great Grandfather, Ben Hale, is by far, one of the greatest men I have ever known. The lives he touched are countless.

He grew up in Petit Jean Mountain, and was one of sixteen children. He was born December 31, 1899, and lived a fulfilled life that would cover a part of three centuries. While he particularly loved horses, he had a healthy understanding and respect for all animals. At the age of sixteen, he was thrown from a horse and broke his hip, crippling him for the rest of his life. Even beyond his crippling experience of being thrown from a horse during that early stage of his life, his love for the horse kept him riding for many years to come. He never complained about anything.

At the age of 21, he left the mountain life behind and moved to North Little Rock, Arkansas, where he eventually owned and operated his own gas station. He married Ida Hale, my Great Grandmother, in 1924. The evening of the day they were married, with fifty cents in his pocket, Ben and Ida were involved in a vehicle accident, crashing his Model T Ford into a tree. They both suffered serious injuries, but recovered to live long, fulfilled lives, eventually giving birth to one daughter, Ruby, my Grandmother. She enjoyed riding and working with the horses by her dad's side, and riding in the parades with him.

I grew up spending a great portion of my younger years at their home. The elementary school I attended was located literally right off of the corner of their backyard, and for many years, my home was right around the block. They picked me up every day after school, and I would typically have my choice of McDonalds or Burger King for my after school snack. I believe that was back in the day when a Happy Meal was twenty-five cents. I remember he had to drive with his legs crossed to operate the vehicle, as one leg was basically useless to him. We would then go to their comfy little home, where I would lay on my towel in front of the television, watching *Andy Griffith*, and *The Beverly Hillbilly's*, while eating my Happy Meal and the absolute best homemade chocolate chip cookies.

My Great Grandfather preserved the history of the mountain he grew up on, as well as the history surrounding his whole life. The stories he shared colorfully recounted the era in which he lived. The stories he would tell me—or anyone with a listening ear—formed many of the precious moments of my favorite childhood memories. I spent many afternoons with him, playing dominoes and listening intently to his stories. He kept his Bible on the table by his lift recliner, and we read out of it every day. There is no telling how many times that man read his Bible from beginning to end. I cherish these memories with every fiber of my being.

Some of the best times of my childhood were spent in their backyard, or on their front porch. One particularly fond memory is of the story he shared with everyone about me pretending the porch was my classroom, teaching him to spell "dog," "cat," and "horse," while writing the three words all over the porch with chalk. I learned a lot from this magnificent man.

He taught me about caterpillars and butterflies, as I witnessed the actual transformation and emergence of the monarch butterfly in his backyard when I was six years old. He taught me about ants and their colonies, how hard they worked as a family, how they worked together as a team to survive. He told me about locusts and why they shed their outer shell, and about snakes and why they shed their skin. He taught me about birds and how they differ from one another.

I am reminded of a particular event, when a baby blue jay had fallen from the neighbor's birdhouse. After the fall, the small bird had gotten caught in the fence, so I ran up to rescue it. My intention was to pick it up and take it to my Great Grandfather so he could fix it. I picked up the bird, and turned to go back to him, and the next thing I knew, I had about fifty birds, all blue jays, screeching at me, landing on my head and pecking at me. My poor Great Grandfather was too crippled to get up to run and save me, so I ran with the baby bird in my hands and put it on the other side of the fence. Once I put it down, I turned and ran faster than I ever had to the safety and comfort of his gentle arms.

He taught me the simple things in life, you know: rocks, trees, water, the air that we breathe, and, most importantly, life. These are our true gifts. He taught me that one could not exist without the other, and how true that actually is. Think about it. Even the first building structure of Christ's church could not have been built without the simple things in life. Every day, these things get taken for granted, while our very existence and survival depends entirely upon them. He also taught me that God's greatest gift was a child. For God gave his only begotten Son that whosoever believeth in Him shall not pass away, but have everlasting life (John 3:16). He taught me that God has given us all gifts to help lead, guide, and direct one another.

My Great Grandfather always loved speaking to the animals and saying things, such as, "Well, hey there little fellow, how are you?" It didn't matter if it was a butterfly, frog, locust, dog or horse, he always referred to them as "little fellow." He clearly had an honest and pure way of not only communicating with animals, but also of truly understanding them. Many times, I recall being told of individuals who would drive my Great Grandfather to look at horses, and that he could tell you all about each horse as soon as he laid eyes on them. It didn't matter if he got out of the vehicle or not. He simply had a gift of knowing the animals.

His gift didn't stop there, though. He communicated with children and adults in the same manner. Oh, how he adored children. And they all adored him as well! I can remember him using his walker to make it down to the bottom of his steep driveway, just to give out candy to the local trash service workers to take home to their children. He would even give candy out to the schoolchildren getting off the school bus near his driveway in the afternoon.

Ultimately, the day came when I received a phone call from my dad, to tell me of my Great Grandfather's passing. I dropped to my knees with tears of such sorrow, such loss and emptiness; yet, I wept for his happiness. Shortly before

Granddad's passing, I was at his bedside, holding his gentle hand as I always did. I had just finished assisting him with his meal. He began reminiscing through our history and his stories, the things he had taught me, where he was going, and what he would leave behind. He prepared me for his inevitable journey.

He spoke of a journey that would lead him to the gates of Heaven, to Jesus Christ, to a place where he would kneel before Him with a crown of jewels. This journey would lead him to an everlasting life with the woman he had missed so terribly. He began to shed tears as he spoke to me of being able to walk again—to walk again with Ida, hand in hand. As he began to squeeze my hand, he assured me, as always, that God had surrounded me with His angels and that I would be all right. He asked me to remember the things he had taught me through his repeated stories. He began to chuckle as he mentioned how sometimes he would repeat his stories because sometimes people didn't "get it" the first time.

He then proceeded to ask me to make a promise. As I clinched his hand and wiped a tear, I calmly told him, "Sure Granddad, anything."

"Never turn your back on a child. Guide and direct them," he made me promise.

Then he reminded me that God's greatest gift to us is a child, just as He had given us His child, Jesus Christ. He asked me to teach children about the animals and to make a difference. I promised to do so. He then reminded me of Philippians 4:13; "I can do all things through Christ which strengtheneth me." This was my last conversation with my Great Grandfather, Ben Hale, one of the many conversations to never be forgotten.

Some years have passed, and scrolling through my own Rolodex, it has become clearer for me to understand what he spent his life believing and teaching. The things he knew, the things he taught us, and what he left behind. Ben Hale exhibited desire, evenness, and dedication in everything I witnessed him do. He didn't walk very well, but he walked the line, a line that we should all walk more. He walked the line of faith and honesty. He humbled himself before the Lord, and strived to live his life as Christlike as he could. He was forgiving and loving.

Ben Hale exhibited the five responsibilities of Alpha as well: Leadership, Guidance, Grace, Compassion, and Understanding. Through his actions, stories and touch, he exhibited these traits to the utmost perfection, not only to our family, but to each person he came into contact with as well, guiding each of us in a way that was true, open, and honest. He was firm, fair and consistent. He was kind with his words, and never out of line. He was a true gentleman. He was content with who he was, and what he had.

Ben Hale communicated by understanding the definition of such being a two way avenue of exchanging thoughts, ideas, and information. He communicated to each of us on a level that could be understood. Ben Hale was a man who trusted, a man of vision and great faith. My relationship with him could not have been any more cohesive.

Since he moved on to take his walk with the Lord at the age of 101 years old, not a day goes by that he is not missed. As each day passes, I seem to learn more from his stories and the example he left behind. I see his traits and characteristics living through my Grandmother and I, as well as those whose lives he touched. I see these traits and characteristics in my children, and I know that my Great Grandfather would be pleased.

In Memory of Ben Hale

1899-2001

He Loved to Ride Horses

CPSIA information can be obtained
at www.ICGtesting.com
Printed in the USA
BVOW08s0834201216
471341BV00001B/23/P

9 780981 651156